STEVEN H. McDONOUGH

Strategy and skill in learning a foreign language

Edward Arnold

A member of the Hodder Headline Group
LONDON NEW YORK SYDNEY AUCKLAND

To my mother, Natalie McDonough

First published in Great Britain 1995 by
Edward Arnold, a division of Hodder Headline PLC,
338 Euston Road, London NW1 3BH

Distributed exclusively in the USA by
St. Martin's Press, Inc.
175 Fifth Avenue, New York, NY 10010

British Library Cataloguing in Publication Data
A catalogue record for this book is available from the British Library

Library of Congress Cataloging-in-Publication Data
A catalog record for this book is available from the Library of Congress

ISBN 0 340 59109 9 (Pb)
ISBN 0 340 62532 5 (Hb)

1 2 3 4 5   95 96 97 98 99

Typeset in 10½/12½ Ehrhardt by
Paston Press Ltd, Loddon, Norfolk
Printed and bound in Great Britain by
J W Arrowsmith Ltd, Bristol

Table of contents

Preface

Recently the notion of strategy, both for language use and for language learning, has attracted a great deal of attention. In this book I have attempted to lay out what is known about strategies for language using and for language learning with reference to second-language learning, to discuss the origin of that knowledge in particular kinds of research on language learners, to show what significance it has for the idea of language skills and the skilled language learner, and to highlight the implications that I see in it for our current views of learning activities in second-language classrooms, and for second-language testing.

The book makes a fairly simple-minded distinction between skill areas in terms of the familiar four skills. I chose this merely as a convenient way of organizing and presenting what is otherwise a quite varied data set, and with no intention of suggesting that actual language behaviour is so neatly compartmentalized. Classroom language learning has largely dispensed with such rigid boundaries in the interests of integrated-skills teaching, and it is evident from the strategy literature that learners voluntarily cross such artificial boundaries in their approach to solving language-learning problems. Nevertheless, there remain interesting differences in the way students cope with problems, for example of compensatory behaviour in talk situations, of teasing out the main ideas of a reading passage, of rehearsing and revising written compositions, and of perceiving what coherence they can find in the many-faceted life of the classroom.

A feature of the book is the use of a considerable number of examples. It is always difficult to work with examples, because so often an example chosen to illustrate one feature under discussion actually illustrates many others at the same time; and because a startling example can sometimes obscure a more general point. Nevertheless, the use of examples allows the respondents – mainly the language learners themselves – to speak for themselves, and one theme of this book is that progress in language-learning research is only possible by finding ways of allowing learners to have their say, even if – or especially if – what they say is idiosyncratic and uncomfortable in terms of the grand, abstract theories of second-language learning or language acquisition.

A related feature is the exploration of the remarkable amount of intro-spective or 'self-revelatory' research now available to complement the quantitative research effort on one side and the programmatic development of methods on the other. This kind of research is not new, though it is now being extended into many areas, such as testing and classroom processes, where other methods have been found unsatisfactory or less insightful than had been hoped. Consequently, some space in the book has been reserved for a discussion of these methods of data collection and analysis.

The book, however, eschews concrete prescriptions 'based on the latest research' for teachers to follow in their classes. More detailed reasons for not doing this are discussed in Chapter 7. I believe that there are many useful implications to be drawn for current practice – for example, for understanding what students are doing and why they succeed sometimes and fail at other times – but I do not believe that it is the role of research in this field to dictate new methods or indeed new constraints on teachers, without careful empirical evaluation of the proposals.

I am very grateful to candidates for Ph.D., MA, Diploma, and Certificate qualifications in the Department of Language and Linguistics and the EFL Unit, at the University of Essex, for listening to drafts of this book and providing valuable argument and feedback during the writing. I am particularly grateful to Jo McDonough for taking on the burden of proof-reading. All the errors that remain are necessarily my own fault.

Steven McDonough
University of Essex
1995

Acknowledgements

I am grateful to the following for permission to quote material:

Paramount Publishing International, for pages 76 and 77 of 'The learning strategies of ESL Students' by Anna Uhl Chamot, in *Learner strategies in language learning*, 1987, edited by Anita Wenden and Joan Rubin, published by Prentice Hall International. EFL Services Ltd., for extracts from their report *Students Talking*, 1992. Multilingual Matters Ltd for the two extracts from 'The use of retrospective verbal reports' by N. Poulisse, T. Bongaerts, and E. Kellerman, in *Introspection in second language research*, 1987, edited by C. Faerch and G. Kasper. Longman Group Ltd for the extracts from C. Hosenfeld's article 'Case studies of ninth grade readers' in *Reading in a foreign language*, 1984, edited by J. C. Alderson and A. H. Urquhart; also for the extract and table from the article 'Achievement strategies in learner/native-speaker interaction' by K. Haastrup and R. Phillipson, in *Strategies in interlanguage communication*, 1983, edited by C. Faerch and G. Kasper. Oxford University Press for the transcript of 'Investigating the reading problems of ESL students' by Yeghia Aslanian in *English Language Teaching Journal*, Vol. 39, No. 1, January 1985. Professor Ellen Block and TESOL for the extracts from 'The comprehension strategies of second language readers' by Ellen Block, *TESOL Quarterly*, Vol. 20, No. 3, 1986, pp. 472–4 and 493–4; copyright 1986 by Teachers of English to Speakers of Other Languages (TESOL); adapted by permission.

1

Strategy, process, and skill in language learning

What this book is about

In very general terms, this book is about what learners of English as a Foreign Language tell us, in all sorts of ways, about the processes of learning the language, and of learning to use the language in various situations and skill areas. Later chapters will draw implications for teaching methodology and the organization of language classes and courses, for testing language proficiency, and evaluating courses and programmes.

However, the scope of the book is not universal. There is already a substantial literature on second- and foreign-language development; the reader need only look as far as Littlewood (1984), Larsen-Freeman and Long (1991), Ellis (1986), and Cook (1991), to see the results of the important research trends in the last twenty years and to find discussion of their implications for, and probable effects on, the practice and organization of language teaching.

This book is more restricted in scope. It is devoted to exploring the kind of information we get from certain types of evidence. Commonly, people distinguish between 'hard evidence' from controlled experimental studies, which tends to be expressed in numbers, and 'soft evidence' from more personal kinds of studies: questionnaires, case studies, self-reports, diaries, observations. Both kinds of evidence can be difficult to interpret, for different reasons. Hard evidence is only as hard as the experimental checks and counterbalances built into the experimental design, and requires very careful interpretation if unwarranted generalizations are to be avoided. Soft evidence is often only from individuals, and is open to doubts concerning the individuals' degree of self-knowledge and the extent to which generalizations are possible at all. Later in this chapter I shall return to this distinction and develop it further. None the less, there are exciting possibilities in looking at what I have termed 'soft' evidence, not least because what people report they believe happens to them affects their future actions, and what they attribute their success or failure to strongly affects their attitudes and motivation in further learning experiences. That is why a major part of the book is about what learners tell us directly about their experience, as well as what they tell us by less direct means.

Plan of the book

In this first chapter, a number of issues need to be explored before we can look at the specific skill areas of English as a Foreign Language and the implications for teaching and testing directly, but with knowledge of the problems of evidence, data collection, and data analysis that surrounds these questions.

We will look at the distinctions to be drawn between strategies, skills, and processes in learning and using language; the difference between processes you can pay attention to and processes you cannot inspect; the notion of heeded processes in terms of how they can be revealed and how they act as conscious springs of action; methods of discovery of those processes and strategies; the controversies surrounding the use of a particular technique, *verbal report*, in general and in language learning; comparison of this kind of data with other sources of information; a foretaste of the implications of this kind of evidence for issues in language education; the question of the user-friendliness of these methods and the possibilities for other language teachers doing some of this kind of research in their own or each others' classes. Subsequent chapters will then look, from the point of view developed in this first chapter, at specific skill areas such as talking (inside and outside class) (Chapter 2); learning to read and listen (Chapter 3); learning to write (Chapter 4); and learning to learn (Chapter 5). Chapter 6 will consider the implications of some of these results and this kind of research methodology for some important questions in testing; Chapter 7 will do the same for the organization of teaching, as regards classroom interaction, participation, attention, methodology, syllabus development, and evaluation.

Preliminary discussions

Strategies, processes, and skills

This group of terms needs some clarification, since they are used in a variety of senses in everyday language and in the language-teaching literature.

Skills

If someone is skilled at something, we tend to think of them as being able to do whatever it is faster, more smoothly, and more successfully than someone who is unskilled. Skills therefore have a number of general features:

1. Performance: skills are about doing things.
2. Specific application: one can be skilled at particular kinds of performance and not others.
   Wide range of performances:
   physical: e.g. sports
   psychomotor: e.g. driving a car, steering a boat, flying
   intellectual: e.g. problem-solving
   interpersonal: persuading, convincing, socializing
   informational: reading.
3. They are amenable to learning and possibly instruction.
4. There are individual differences in level of achievement.
5. Performance is smooth, sensitive to feedback, integrated in time.
6. Most of the time, skills lead to success.

In discussion of language skills it has long been commonplace to refer to the various modes of language performance as skills; speaking, reading, writing, and listening (the four-skills approach of Audio-Lingualism). But it is evident that such terms are very general, and not quite consonant with the use of ordinary language – and the literature on skill acquisition within psychology – or 'skill' in specific applications. Hence it is nowadays convenient to refer also to subskills – for example, Nuttall's (1982) use of the division between word-attack skills and text-attack skills in her discussion of teaching foreign-language reading.

We shall have cause to return to this distinction later in the discussion of reading, but for the present it is important to notice that there is no generally agreed or empirically justified analysis of what subskills or component skills actually exist in the intellectual or cognitive field. Indeed, psychologists working in the field of mental testing have been looking for most of this century for a satisfactory way of analysing such skills, often using the complicated techniques of factor analysis to divine where tests appear to be testing the same trait and where they do not.

Processes

Of the three concepts, process is the simplest and yet the most overused. A process is the mechanism by which a set of information is transformed: thus the writing process is the mechanism by which ideas are transformed into characters on a page. The term at that level of generality hides a number of important issues, however. Cognitive processes occur through time, and are thus subject to constraints of real time such as overload and memory; and they may occur in linear order, as in a model of writing which specifies a series of stages from thought through outline to expression, or in parallel, as when several elements of a process occur simultaneously, for example in the activation of vocabulary and vocabulary associations such as synonyms and antonyms.

Strategies

This term is currently enjoying a vogue in language-learning circles, with a variety of implications. There are four broad categories of meaning.

An organizing principle or policy: Governments are repeatedly castigated for reacting to events with short-term measures rather than having a long-term strategy: thus in this sense strategy is an articulated plan for meeting particular types of problems, not a piece of problem-solving in itself.

An alternative to calculation by rule: Psychologists occasionally speak of strategies when referring to human mental ploys which appear to be used when alternative methods entail penalties of cognitive overload, memory, or knowledge. Thus Bever (1970) suggested that while acquiring language children used a strategy to recognize certain kinds of grammatical forms which gave a good answer most of the time, just as a bird-watcher counting a flock of geese in flight may estimate how many groups of five he can see (the 'span of apprehension') because counting one by one would take longer than the geese are apparent to the eye.

Compensation: A large part of the literature in second-language studies has focused on the use of strategies for overcoming communication breakdown. Tarone (1981), Varadi (1980), Faerch and Kasper (1983*b*), and Bialystok (1990) have all tried to clarify the increasingly difficult problem of how learners cope with the situation where they have a meaning to transmit or receive, but lack the normal linguistic means of encoding that meaning. Bialystok (1990) devotes two chapters to 'defining' and 'identifying' communication strategies, reviewing in the process the arguments put forward by the other authors. She discusses various proposals for defining criteria for strategies, and their potential for separating strategic and non-strategic behaviour, showing that each is less than adequate. For example, strategies are used when there is a problem, a breakdown; but, she points out, this does not mean that strategies cannot be used where there is not a problem, unless the notion of problem is so reduced in force as to mean any translation between meaning and form of language. A learner might use the strategy of avoidance (Tarone, 1981) if expressing what he wanted to express was going to be just too difficult – an instance of *problematicity*. However, both a learner and a native speaker might choose a strategy of describing a biological specimen from the centre to the periphery, or from the periphery to the centre, where neither would necessarily tax their linguistic resources but a choice has to be made (Urquhart, 1984). A second proposal Bialystok discusses is *consciousness*. It is often assumed that people are aware of the strategic choices they make; but this is not necessarily so, nor can it be shown to be necessarily true. A third one is *intentionality*, and it is implicit in the idea of conscious choice; however, Bialystok argues that there is little evidence for this feature in the empirical studies of strategy use in second-language performance. However, Bialystok does advance three other features which occur in most of the discussions about strategy use, and summarizes her approach thus (1990: 12):

> First, strategies are effective: they are related to solutions in specific ways, and they are productive in solving the problem for reasons which theorists can articulate. Second, strategies are systematic: learners do not create or stumble upon the best strategy for solving a problem but uncover the strategy from their knowledge of the problem and employ it systematically. Third, strategies are finite: a limited number of strategies can be identified. Strategies are not idiosyncratic creations of learners. Larger structures, which some call executive control structures, provide a context for organizing strategies into more general skills that are applicable to a range of problems. This systematicity of strategies should be kept as a guiding factor in the search for descriptions and explanations of the strategies used by second language learners.

Plans: A fourth way of conceiving of strategies is to think of them as plans for action. In the literature of learning strategies there have been a number of attempts to set up general principles which may describe the kinds of plan that successful language learners use. This tradition goes back to the work of Stern (1975) and Rubin (1975), who attempted to specify plans of action whose use might distinguish successful language learners from unsuccessful ones. Stern's original ten strategies – 'features that mark out good language learning' (1975: 31) – are as follows:

1. A personal learning style or positive learning strategies;
2. An active approach to the learning task;
3. A tolerant and outgoing approach to the target language and empathy with its speakers;
4. Technical know-how about how to tackle a language;
5. Strategies of experimentation and planning with the object of developing the new language into an ordered system and of revising this system progressively;
6. Constantly searching for meaning;
7. Willingness to practise;
8. Willingness to use the language in real communication;
9. Self-monitoring and critical sensitivity to language use;

10. Developing the target language more and more as a separate reference system, and learning to think in it.

This use of strategy is probably closest to the first, ordinary language
sense, except that it is not tied directly to problem-solving. It is, rather, a
set of wholesome attitudes. Faerch and Kasper (1983b), however, explicitly
reject the equation of strategy and plan, talking again about communication
strategies, and attempt to draw a sharp distinction between them based
on the difference between a planning phase of problem-solving and an
execution phase: strategies operate to put into effect the decisions
embodied in the plan. Bialystok (1990) points out that this distinction is
difficult to maintain.

This brief discussion will most likely have given the impression that the
concept of psychological strategy is a very difficult one to pin down in a
clear fashion that can be accepted by a majority of workers in the field.
This impression is quite justified; and yet it does not prevent this undeniably useful notion from continuing to be used both as a programmatic principle, i.e. as a justification for certain kinds of teaching, for example in
'learner training', and as an explanatory principle, for example in studies of
communication breakdown and individual differences in learning. It will
recur many times in various guises in the test that follows. A number of
questions will have to be addressed:

- How can strategies be identified and verified?
- Can they be isolated and empirically demonstrated?
- Can one distinguish between strategic and non-strategic beha-
  viour?
- Do communication strategies become learning strategies?
- Do strategies change during development?

Processes that you can pay attention to and processes that you can't

Although in the above discussion Bialystok was quoted as dismissing the
feature of consciousness as a defining criterion of the concept of strategy,
the idea that there are some processes in language use that the user has
awareness of and some that are not available to conscious inspection
remains a popular one. Although its use in language learning can be traced
at least as far back as Palmer's (1964 [1922]) distinction between studial
and spontaneous learning, the formulation that has created the most
impact in recent times has been Krashen's (1977) distinction between
'learning' and 'acquisition'. Krashen suggested that these two processes
were distinguished by their availability to conscious awareness, as well as
by a number of other criteria such as focus on accuracy or fluency and time
for response. The criterion of conscious awareness, hotly debated by
McLaughlin (1978), for example, had two implications. First, learning is

available to be reported on, so that, for example, a rule which the student has understood can be recalled and used as an editing device (the Monitor); but the kinds of rule that can be so treated are limited to those few that can be easily formulated. Second, learning is voluntary and is controlled by the will, whereas acquisition, being what young children do to acquire their first language, is involuntary, and will occur wherever there are examples of the language for the acquisition system to work on, as happens to young children learning the language of their natural environment. It followed from Krashen's formulation that learning processes could be paid attention to, be heeded, by the learner, whereas acquisition processes could not be. Krashen's distinction fell foul of a number of criticisms concerned with his failure to provide any kind of detailed account of acquisition, and his rather quirky definition of learning as what occurs in formal situations, where there is both isolation of rules (as in a structural syllabus) and the presence of feedback or error correction; such criticisms are detailed in many publications such as McLaughlin (1987) and Ellis (1986).

A more recent version of the same distinction is emerging from work in the Universal Grammar approach to second-language development. Here Krashen's somewhat cavalier definition of an 'acquisition' process is replaced by a richer, though equally unconscious and involuntary, notion. Data from the language are used to decide on the values (called Parameters) attached to certain crucial aspects of all human languages (called Universal Grammatical Principles) in the particular case of the language the child is encountering. For these theorists (White, 1986; Flynn, 1989; Cook, 1991) the acquisition process uses three kinds of information: innate knowledge of the defining principles of human language, facts about the syntax of the language encountered, and facts about the normal syntactic privileges of words in the language.

Thus, a central area of what has to be mastered in the new language is assigned by this theory to an automatic process, whose activity is 'triggered' by encountering certain kinds of evidence from the language in question, conceivably in remarkably small quantities. Cook (1989: 171) points out that this theory has nothing to say about 'learning strategies, motivations, cognitive or social schemas, or whatever', nor variability, teacher talk, interaction, practice, explanation of rules, or error correction. Indeed, it is conspicuous that, according to this article, the language-teaching and language-learning concerns to which the Universal Grammar approach is not relevant considerably outweigh those to which it is. The controversies surrounding this theoretical position, both within linguistics and among language-teaching researchers (see the articles by Gass and Bley-Vroman in Gass and Schachter, 1989) are not particularly important as regards the central theme of this book, which is devoted to evidence of a different kind, that emanating directly or indirectly from learners about those areas of language development which are, apparently, not addressed by the very limited contribution of Universal Grammar. We should remember, in passing, that the use of such terms as 'triggering', 'switching', and 'decision-making' is purely by analogy with their normal, real-world, voluntary referents; the operation of a Universal Grammar contribution is by definition involuntary, automatic, self-governing, and not available for attentional processes. There is, of course, an argument as to where the dividing line occurs, and whether a dividing line is accepted at all; this appears particularly in discussion of feedback and error correction by teachers on grammatical and lexical forms produced by learners, both in the form of the teachers' identification of the place and nature of an error and the students' acceptance and processing of the information. Universal Grammar theory would appear to represent a claim that this is irrelevant; both teachers and learners appear to regard it as a major component of the teaching/learning process. The issue is even more profiled in the case of student-initiated clarification and comprehension checks, which are characteristic of both native and learner discourse. The problem for an integrated theory of language learning is whether a heeded, attention-attracting process or strategy can affect an unheeded, automatic one; in psychology it is an old problem referred to as 'incidental' or 'latent' learning.

It is also possible to draw a distinction between processes that can be heeded and those that cannot, within particular skill areas or modes of language use. In reading, for instance, we shall see that certain processes seem to be talked about and reported to the exclusion of others: thus, certain strategies and decisions involving high-level ('top-down') features such as argument and perception of author's intention seem to be available for conscious review, while for mature native readers, processes of decoding the text ('bottom-up') into syntactic constituents and semantic units do not.

Heeded processes as conscious springs of action

The argument addressed here is that the beliefs and mental processes learners report in questionnaires, diaries, and verbal reports, and the strategies that can be inferred from cases of conversation breakdown and negotiation of meaning, constitute valid data which are necessary for a full understanding of how second-language development progresses and in what ways it varies from individual to individual. This is neither original nor controversial; it is in the tradition of psychological approaches to second-language development (SLD) stretching back to Beliaev (1963), McDonough (1981), and Skehan (1989). An important concern, however, is how these activities contribute to development. An assumption which is implicit in the approach described in this book is that processes that you can focus attention on, and strategies that you can adopt voluntarily, are activities which you can review and evaluate; therefore, they affect motivation, choice of future action, attributions of responsibility, by normal cognitive processes that are familiar in areas other than language learning, and are demonstrated in cognitive approaches to, for example, skill acquisition (Anderson, 1983) and motivation (Weiner, 1972). This is not to claim that unheeded processes cannot have an effect; it is to say that what we believe we are doing, what we pay attention to, what we think is important, how we choose to behave, how we prefer to solve problems, form the basis for our personal decisions as to how to proceed. An important fact about this argument is that it is not necessary for these kinds of evidence to be true for them to have important consequences for our further development. It is quite possible, indeed, as a literary commonplace, part of the human condition, that the evidence on which we base our future action is sometimes invalid and untrue. As rational human beings, we may assume that the more accurate our perceptions, the more likely our decisions are going to be correct. Hence, in language-learning circles we have the strong trend towards accurate self-monitoring and self-evaluation in approaches as far apart as Curran's 'Community language learning' (1976), Ellis and Sinclair's 'Learner training' (1989), Dickinson's 'Self-instruction' (1987), and Oskarson's 'Self-assessment' (1984).

How can we find out what other learners can tell us?

Research methods in second-language development and second-language teaching are diverse, with both numerical and qualitative methods, and hard and soft evidence, featuring strongly. In fact, the whole question of appropriate research methods is the subject of growing debate associated with particular arguments about the aims and utility of language teaching and learning research (cf. McDonough and McDonough, 1993; Allwright and Bailey, 1991; Larsen-Freeman and Long, 1991; Nunan, 1992; Seliger and Shohamy, 1989). In the category of soft evidence, we can usefully distinguish between *indirect* methods, such as

- questionnaires
- discourse analysis
- check inventories

involving either the learners' agreement or disagreement with certain proposals or the researcher's inference of certain strategic decisions from specified kinds of behaviour, and *direct* methods,

- protocol analysis
- self-revelation
- diaries
- verbal report
- interview

in which typically the learner is asked for an account in a semi-structured or unstructured fashion about what he was paying attention to or observed himself doing while performing some language tasks like reading, writing, talking to people in certain ways, and even listening.

Both kinds of evidence are useful for research in skills, strategies, and processes: each kind of data has its own limitations. For example, questionnaires have their place in determining people's attitudes and beliefs about what they want and what they believe they will do, or have done; they cannot tell us what they actually do. They can also be analysed numerically by correlation and cross-tabulation. By the same token, a protocol or commentary can give us valuable information on what is going through the mind of an individual while she writes a composition; but it can tell us nothing about what the writer does not pay attention to, and poses considerable interpretation problems. They can also be analysed in rather crude numerical terms, as frequencies of particular categories or strategies, and in certain cases as sequences of activities over time. However, the value of both direct and indirect kinds of evidence is primarily the quality of the insights they afford, particularly into an individual's behaviour; moreover, some of these insights cannot be gained by any other means.

Using verbal reports

Using verbal reports – asking people to tell us in language what they believe they are doing when they perform certain skills, learning tasks, or whatever – has a long history in both psychology and social science, though in some ways it has been something of a fringe activity. It has only recently been introduced into second-language learning research. In general, it was regarded as a useful source of hypotheses about mental processes but not as an admissible kind of evidence for verification of those hypotheses. In other words, it could be used as a source of ideas but not as a test of those ideas. Nisbett and Wilson (1977), in a much-quoted review, argued that verbal reports could not be used as evidence for the validity of the processes they reflected, for several reasons. First, people's observation of their own behaviour is notoriously unreliable: people believe they do things for reasons which are often spurious, while a simple explanation (like habit, or conformity to perceived group pressures) is not admitted. Second, there are obvious limits on the degree of 'depth' of process and mental computation to which people have access by conscious attention. Third, the act of expressing these perceptions in language, actually making the verbal report, may considerably alter the performance of the task, compared with occasions when they are merely performing the task without making a report.

These arguments smack of the distinction between science and common sense highlighted by Lewis Wolpert and briefly reported in *The Guardian* (29 October 1992). Wolpert argues that science is essentially unnatural: it is anything but 'trained common sense'. One might ask, therefore, what we are doing in language education advocating looking again at what our fallible learners report in various ways about what they do. The answer is, of course, that our beliefs about ourselves and our world – our common sense – are the product of our experience and, in Wolpert's words, provide 'an excellent basis for day-to-day living'. The process of education is not a magical, non-participatory activity – it is everyday living. The point of studying such reports and perceptions of processes and activities in education is precisely to subject this mass of insights to scientific analysis and thereby acknowledge the richness of people's language-learning experiences, rather than reducing it to only those aspects which are amenable to study by particular experimental means.

Ericson (1988) and Ericson and Simon (1987) have argued that the Nisbett and Wilson criticisms are not in fact inconsistent with the idea of the value of verbal reports. They point out that, just as with any other kind of data, it is crucial to establish the limits of applicability. Thus, they argue that people can only report what they can pay attention to, which introduces the concept of 'heeded processes'. In itself, that is not to deny that there are processes which are not available for attention. Attention itself has limits: it varies over time and has severe constraints on the number of contemporary events it can handle. There are also limitations on memory and comprehensiveness. This has implications for the method of data collection: many moments of reporting while performing a task are to be preferred to a summative report given after a long task.

Ericson points out that some mental events may be easily coded in language, whereas others may be difficult to express: so-called 'Level 1' and 'Level 2' reporting. With non-native speakers there is the additional complication of giving reports in a less than fluent language. Many of the studies to be mentioned later in the book in fact ask informants to report in their native language, in order to solve this problem. This is only a partial solution, however, because giving a verbal report in your native language about something you are doing in your foreign language may affect your operation in that foreign language.

A crucial issue in using verbal reports as data is whether giving a verbal report actually alters the process being reported on. This is a difficulty not encountered by survey and questionnaire methods, because they do not interfere in time with the activity under scrutiny – indeed, they may be taken at some remove from the activity. Thus one can be sceptical about their claim to truth as opposed to belief or good intentions. Retrospective verbal reporting – telling somebody what you remember doing in, for example, a diary – suffers the same problem of credibility as these indirect methods. However, concurrent verbal reporting usually means doing something – talking about the job while you are doing it – which is not normally done. Several studies have attempted to validate concurrent verbal reporting. Early studies of the problem focused on the reports – called 'protocols' – of people talking their way through solving quasi-mathematical problems or 'brain-teasers' as used by Newell and Simon (1972) in their research into cognitive processes. From these studies, comparing people talking through their solutions to problems and people performing silently, it was concluded that the actual steps people take to solve the problems are the same under both conditions; but talking aloud reveals these steps and decisions overtly. The crucial question then becomes: to what extent can one expect the same finding when looking at real-life second-language tasks such as extracting information from text, generating text, and deciding how best to formulate a speech act? From studies comparing reading aloud with reading silently, where skilled readers comprehend as much by either method but take longer to complete the text when reading aloud, Ericson (1988) concludes that giving a concurrent verbal report may slow down but not change the process.

Smagorinsky (1989), in an article considering the objections to verbal report on the writing process, highlights three important issues:

Does a verbal report change the process being reported on?

This issue is the one that led us into the discussion of problems in using verbal reports. In this context Smagorinsky quotes an apparently damning study by Berkenkotter (1983), comparing protocols from an established professional writer writing in his normal, rather idiosyncratic manner, with him writing and talking into a tape-recorder with herself present as an observer. In the second situation the subject immediately became totally tongue-tied and suffered writer's block. However, the test of the verbal-report method was itself artificial, with a very challenging set topic and a subject with a lifetime's habit of writing in a particular way. Smagorinsky therefore discounts Berkenkotter's evidence.

The significance of gaps

Information from protocols is bound to be incomplete, in the sense that nobody can verbalize every decision in a complex hierarchical process. This is no more a criticism of verbal protocol research than of any kind of research where data is necessarily limited: if anything, verbal reports suffer from the opposite, being too rich. Times when informants dry up and cannot say anything may, however, indicate something rather different: for example, that the combined cognitive load of performing the task and talking about it is too high to be doing both. Under such circumstances, an informant may simply not say anything while he or she solves the problem in hand. Cooper and Holzmann (1983) have argued that this kind of data cannot be used for building models of the writing process (see Chapter 4) precisely because one cannot go beyond the data and infer processes that are not reported. However, that is precisely what more obviously 'scientific', experimental approaches do, in order to choose between theoretical accounts on the basis of quantitative data.

Data from verbal reports needs to be substantiated by comparison with other evidence

This issue will recur several times, and is sometimes termed 'triangulation'. Verbal reports of reading can be compared with measures of reading comprehension; statistical-test validity measures can be compared with what candidates say about the items; diary entries can be compared with class observation. Cohen (1992: 135) has summarized the various approaches to retrospective reporting, delayed reporting, concurrent reporting, directed reporting, and so on, in his trio of

- self-report
- self-observation
- self-revelation.

Individual reports in second-language learning

Retrospective reporting has been used in various studies of language learning. Pickett (1978) asked a number of experienced language learners to reflect on what they remembered of how they had learned their languages. He reported a list of forty 'prompts' to see if they produced any agreement; the number of features highlighted by the respondents rose to 108, nearly twice as many again as his original list. Fairfax and Green (1989) studied reports written by students about their learning of *ab initio* Russian as part of their language studies degree. This data has considerable diversity and richness, but it is limited because the reports were submitted in partial fulfilment of a degree assessment scheme. Bailey and Ochsner (1983) have looked at a number of diaries written by language learners, including themselves, to assess their value and limitations. Bailey's own study (1980) of competitiveness and anxiety growing in herself as she underwent a language learning course remains a classic in the field. Schmidt and Frota (1986) report on Schmidt's participation in learning Portuguese by attending classes, and highlight the frustrations at the tasks demanded of them by the teacher – a theme that also recurs frequently in the reports reviewed by Fairfax and Green. Reactions by students to teaching techniques and contrasting evaluations by students and teachers of methods will be an important part of our discussion of teaching implications in Chapter 7.

Some possible implications

The chapters that follow will attempt to present (within the acknowledged limitations of the data available and the specific constraints on interpretation of the particular kind of data being used) the implications which these direct and indirect sources of information about language learning suggest, for a number of themes:

Language awareness

What language learners imagine language is like, what sensitivities they have, what use of language knowledge they make.

Learner awareness

What they perceive learning a language to be like, and what they compare it with. How they view the process of teaching and what they can tell us about being on the receiving end of tests.

Learner training

What evidence there might be that training students to learn in certain ways, to adopt certain attitudes, to emphasize certain behaviours, might increase their language proficiency: in short, whether people can learn to learn languages, and whether poor learners can learn to be good ones.

Learner centredness

What the effect on learners themselves is of learner-centred teaching. Methods of evaluating the effectiveness of learner-centred teaching, in particular by asking learners for their perceptions and opinions.

Teacher awareness

The extent to which teachers can and do reveal their professional assumptions and craft knowledge through this kind of evidence, and the relevance of this for the evaluation of teaching, teacher development, and teacher training.

Evaluation of programmes

Product measures – scores on tests – have long been used to evaluate the effectiveness of teaching, with varying success. Questionnaire data is often used as one element in the evaluation of a teaching programme, as it is for the assessment of individual teachers. The dangers of equating popularity with effectiveness is, naturally, ever-present. Other forms of learner self-reports may also be relevant for programme evaluation.

User-friendliness of these research methods

The last issue to be raised in this chapter is the possibility of teachers using these kinds of methods and data in their own research. The notion of the teacher as a researcher has been popular – or, at least, lip-service has frequently been paid to it in language learning – since the radical suggestions of Stenhouse (1975), made practical by Hopkins (1993) and Walker (1985). Quite recently it has received considerable impetus in TEFL in the work of Nunan (1992) and Allwright and Bailey's (1991) concept of the 'exploratory classroom'. Whereas a teacher's resources of time and specialist knowledge may be severely stretched by embarking on a piece of research in the classroom in the classical, quantitative, psycho-linguistic mode, the gathering of verbal reports, diary material, answers to questionnaires, and the like, even with due attention to the methodological problems mentioned earlier, is not as daunting.

Moreover, it is likely to be more revealing of their own students' perceptions, strategies, and component skills of learning and communication. Such research may be carried out collaboratively, and the results fed back into decisions about the methods, materials, organizations, and nature of the programme. In this way, educational change may take place 'at the coalface' on the basis of locally conducted empirical research. This may be a pipe-dream; but given the general perception of other kinds of language-learning and teaching research as irrelevant, inaccessible, and often too late, it may be the only way forward.

2

Strategies for talking

Learners talking

There is a large body of research literature available nowadays on the patterns and regularities of student and teacher talk in the classroom, and a substantial, though smaller, body containing descriptions of talk between learners, and between learners and proficient speakers in 'natural' settings outside classrooms. Some of this work has a pedagogic focus, identifying pedagogic tactics, attempting to isolate features of effective teaching; some has a learning focus, identifying patterns of student participation and relating them to possible learning outcomes; some has a communicative focus, inferring learners' ways of managing their linguistic interaction. Much of this work is concerned with what people said: their linguistic products, so to speak, rather than how they came to say it, or their linguistic processes. In what follows, we shall be looking as clearly as possible at these processes, in so far as they are available to the speakers' attention or can be inferred validly.

The questions that need to be answered are the following:

- How do learners plan and monitor what they say in the classroom and in other conversational situations?
- How do learners manage when they sense they cannot express what they want to say?
- How do learners react to feedback?
- What do learners pay attention to?
- What do learners reveal about how they use the language they are learning?

Early work

One of the earliest pieces of research to enquire what learners actually did when asked to perform in class was carried out by Carol Hosenfeld in the early 1970s. Hosenfeld conducted semi-structured interviews with students learning French in New York State. She asked them to tell her how they achieved the right answers on simple transformation exercises set by the teacher. The answers revealed a surprisingly widespread use of sensible strategies for getting the right answer, as if the exercises set some kind of linguistic problem which had to be accomplished by some means or other. For example, here is a student ('Julie') performing a simple transformation task (replace the noun object with a pronoun and adjust agreement) in French (Hosenfeld, 1976: 122):

1. *Ils ont perdu les bérets verts*
2. *Elle a vendu la maison*
3. *J'ai regardé les beaux tableaux*

INTERVIEWER: Let's go on to the next exercise. Would you tell me what you are thinking as you complete number one.

JULIE: Well ... I look at the underlined part first ... put the *les* in front of the verb and add 's' to *perdu*.

INTERVIEWER: Why did you add 's' and not 'es'?

JULIE: Because *verts* is masculine.

INTERVIEWER: Did you look at *bérets* in the underlined part?

JULIE: No. You just need *les* and *verts* ... on number two I look at *la*, put *l'* in front of *a* and add *e* to *vendu*. On three ... I look at *les; beaux* is masculine, otherwise it would be *belle*, and I put *les* in front of the verb ... and add 's' to *regardé*. I don't pay any attention to what the sentence is saying ... I just look for the *le, la, les*, put it in front of the verb, and if it's *les* I look at the adjective a little bit.

Other examples of Hosenfeld's collection of 'think-aloud' interviews demonstrate a wide variety of strategies and attitudes. Some students find simple ways of solving the problem, but their success is not valuable (p. 16):

INTERVIEWER: Why don't you like this stuff?

PEGGY: Well ... because I'm a pretty verbal person ... mixing up the sentence and moving the pieces around ... it's just frustrating to have to continually do this ... and after a while you don't even know what all of this stuff means. I know what the directions are and I know what I'm supposed to do, but I don't know *why* I'm supposed to be doing it ... That bothers me.

Others know perfectly well what to do but refuse to play along, doing their own thing instead. Cora's achievement was to pass all the quizzes, ending up with an A grade, without doing any of the exercises as set: she chose to take the problem given and make up her own sentences. She readily admitted to not doing any of the class exercises, so the interviewer asks her to show her how she studies (Hosenfeld, 1979: 602):

INTERVIEWER: What did you do in class today?

CORA: I read the boxes, I studied the grammar, and I took a test.

INTERVIEWER: Can you show me how you study the grammar?
CORA: (she turns to the following grammar explanation in her text.)

Voilà quelques exemples d'expressions de doute et de possibilité qui gouvernent le subjonctif quand il y a un changement du sujet: il est possible, impossible, douteux, vraisemblable, invraisemblable

I read the expressions and I make my own sentences. I read *Il est possible* and I say *Il est possible que Kurt finisse le livre. Il est douteux; Il est douteux que Steve finisse le livre* ...

INTERVIEWER: What are you thinking as you say the sentences?
CORA: Do you mean do I translate?
INTERVIEWER: Yes
CORA: No, I keep them in French.

Interestingly, her own sentences are about her fellow pupils in this instance. Both Peggy and Cora were clearly anticipating some of the tenets of communicative language teaching long before their time: creation of language and expressing their own thoughts rather than imposed patterns. Perhaps Peggy and Cora were particularly bright or tenacious pupils: others in Hosenfeld's samples showed less independence, but no less individuality. One, Louise, clearly fails to understand the rubrics, which were in the foreign language, a feature that annoyed the independent-minded Peggy, but does claim to pay great attention to them. In point of fact she confesses at the end to resorting to a quite different strategy (Hosenfeld, 1976; 126):

INTERVIEWER: Are directions often difficult to understand?
LOUISE: Yes
INTERVIEWER: What do you usually do?
LOUISE: I ... try to remember how we did it in class.

Whether these exercises required a written or a spoken response, it is quite clear that the students had found adequate ways of achieving the correct answer using clues in the orthography and information from the grammar book. Moreover, these statements by the students quoted by Hosenfeld show a fairly 'cool' assessment of how deeply they need to process the exercise material before finding all the information needed for an answer: hardly ever as deep as the meaning of the sentence. Subsequent research by Hosenfeld investigated the reading strategies. I shall return to the work on reading in a foreign language in Chapter 3. Hosenfeld's work on classroom exercises and grammar learning raised a number of interesting issues which are worth highlighting at this point before we look at more recent work on students talking.

1. Most of the students were successful at performing the exercises, and had ready-made ways of attacking each example of the exercise. In this sense they had a strategy available.

2. From the evidence, it is easy to specify what the strategy was: the students identified the particular information demand of each item and knew where to look and what to do; for example if the article is plural, the adjective carries the gender information.

3. Although these students were being successful, they may not have been learning anything relating directly to how a native speaker would have performed the same task, if ever required to: a native speaker would have probably associated grammatical gender with the noun – with the head rather than the governed.

4. There is no way of knowing whether this way of solving the problem set by the exercise would have changed, as the students' proficiency grew, to a more generally useful strategy. Strategies employed by novices and those employed by experts may differ considerably.

5. It is not clear that anything would be gained by teaching the unsuccessful students the strategies of the successful ones. As Hosenfeld comments in relation to Louise: 'What would be accomplished by replacing an inappropriate strategy with an expedient but useless one?' (1976: 126).

6. One might object that these students are the product of a particular educational culture which puts value on independence while asking its pupils to act in regimented ways, and similar responses to theirs should not be expected from pupils in other cultures. This is perfectly true; but it does not mean that those pupils from other cultures do not have their own opinions which could be solicited.

7. Motivation for this kind of investigation, which is in a sense anarchic and pre-theoretical, may be found in Hosenfeld's comment: 'Too often our focus has been on what students *should be doing*; we must begin by asking what students *are doing*' (1976: 128).

Strategy use in classrooms

Hosenfeld's study was conducted with individual students, not sitting in a class at the time. Her interviews were necessarily, therefore, retrospective in the sense that she was asking the students to tell her what they normally did when faced with these exercises in class. However, Hosenfeld was not able to observe these strategies in operation in real classes, nor question the students when they were actually performing these exercises in a real classroom situation with other students and a teacher present. A study by Cohen and Aphek (1981) attempted to do just that. In this study, the researchers sat in on over twelve hours of class sessions to observe, and also to intervene, to find out what the learners could tell them just after something particularly interesting had happened in the class: as they describe it (p. 227),

moments in which the students made a particularly revealing type of error, achieved striking success, or paused in confusion; as well as moments when the student–teacher interaction led to student confusion possibly resulting in erroneous utterances.

The researchers intended to ask the learners questions as soon after such a 'moment' had occurred as possible – usually in a break, sometimes the next day, occasionally by stopping the class then and there. Such an intrusive researcher presence certainly could be expected to have reactive effects: to have the flow of a class stopped while a student is asked a question is to put at risk the teacher's plan and the students' attention to the subject-matter. Cohen and Aphek acknowledge that this procedure was highly disruptive, and also that in any case the teachers resented their students being observed. We are not told what the students felt, given that they were going to be asked, perhaps in plenary, why they did some particular thing or committed an error.

Cohen and Aphek found that the majority of their interventions in fact concerned errors of various sorts, and they attempted to isolate through questioning the strategies that led to the errors. They comment that it was much easier to identify errors than moments of exceptional success, speculating that this might have been related to the general low level of participation by the students in classroom talk. This cannot be verified, but in general it may also be true that success in classroom tasks is less salient and less well defined than error or failure, and therefore a more private and less publicly remarkable phenomenon in today's classroom culture.

What makes a good strategy?

Cohen and Aphek complicate their report by distinguishing between good, neutral, and bad communicative strategies, but present no independent criteria for acceptability, such as association with eventual success or failure.

The four neutral strategies (guessing, transfer, unanalysed material, and pre-planning) depend for their acceptability on other characteristics of the learner, for example controlled use of knowledge and proficiency level. Thus, guessing is good if the learner typically guesses in a well-informed manner; if it is a substitute for using language and other knowledge to plug the gap, it is less praiseworthy. Another example given by Cohen and Aphek concerns pre-planning. One student reported abandoning a preplanned form when she decided to say something slightly different: but the new phrase required the same form, thus leading to an error of omission. Another student reported his strategy for planning whole sentences before speaking, and his belief that the concern for sentence frames and vocabulary caused him to ignore a detailed morphophonemic matter: elision between preposition and article in Hebrew. Thus pre-planning for these two students led to errors which for different reasons they failed to correct but for which they had clear explanations. Also, acceptability may vary with proficiency level: guessing may be a good strategy for a novice but a poor strategy for a more experienced learner. Successful strategy use may also depend on deeper characteristics of the learner: one of their examples is field independence v. dependence, where field dependence is defined as distraction by material in the immediate context. In this particular example, a student was trying to make sense of the Hebrew words for rich and poor, and misunderstood a word in the teacher's question as a negative – 'not much money' instead of as the resumptive pronoun 'to him'.

Cohen and Aphek's work raises a number of interesting questions, as it reveals some of the ways in which strategies and strategy use resist systematization, despite Bialystok's claim quoted in Chapter 1. An example of a good strategy for them is word coinage. This learner of Hebrew in the class produced a non-word:

*Where do I get off the bus? 'eyfo ani *yariya?'* (should be *ered*)

and explained that in the absence of proper control of the form of the verb she had found a street name apparently derived from the same verb and invented a form based on that. This example shows that adoption of a strategy to compensate for a known deficiency in one's competence requires at least three elements:

1. a choice of solution – in this case making up a form for the verb
2. a source for the solution – in this case an observation which may or may not have been true and relevant
3. a belief that speakers will be able to recognize the result.

Furthermore, two of these elements are constant (otherwise there could be no talk of strategic behaviour, merely of *ad hoc* problem-solving), and one, the source, is variable: it is unlikely that this or any other student would assume that in a similar situation they would rely on another chance observation, but they might nevertheless use the word-coinage strategy.

It is perhaps not surprising that in the intervening decade and a half these authors' challenge to more orthodox classroom observation methodology and error analysis has not been taken up by many subsequent writers: the disruption to the normal flow of classroom procedure is evident, and the reactive effect of questioning the students on their learning is difficult to estimate. However, it established

(*a*) the need to enquire beyond the observable to obtain more detailed knowledge of what was observed (Cohen and Aphek, 1981: 233):

> The important point is that if the purpose of observation is to find out what the learners are doing (thinking, processing, etc.) then classroom observation needs to be coupled with more interventionist tactics such as getting students to introspect (or retrospect at short range).

(*b*) before we can recommend strategies that are 'good' for learning, the determinants of success must be known: the kind of learner for whom it might work; the stage of learning (or proficiency level) it is most suited to; possibly the category of linguistic element (verb form or noun, morphology or syntax).

An early study by Cohen and Robbins (1976) had attempted to isolate learners' errors, learner characteristics, and learner explanations. This study was primarily addressed to one of the main faults in an influential movement in second-language learning research, 'error analysis'. Error analysis (Corder, 1967; Selinker, 1972) had mainly remained at a classificatory level; Cohen and Robbins gave a number of examples which implied that in order to understand an error or a class of errors, and to understand how the error-full performance of a novice becomes the error-free performance of the expert, it was necessary to take into account other kinds of evidence. The two kinds they isolated were individual differences between learners, and the learners' own beliefs about what caused them to commit the errors. The slightly bizarre methodology of Cohen and Aphek's study can best be understood in the light of this previous work.

Taxonomies of strategies used in talk

In the late 1970s and early 1980s there occurred considerable development in the notions of communication, learning, and compensatory strategies (Varadi, 1980; Tarone, 1981; Bialystok, 1990; Faerch and Kasper, 1983*b*; 1987). Most of this work was based on recording and analysis of learner language, and some, but not all, also asked the learners themselves what they thought lay behind the use of strategies.

In a series of papers (1977; 1980; 1981) Tarone gradually refined her notion of communication strategy and differentiated such strategies from those for perception, learning, and production. The four kinds of strategy have different purposes, but this does not mean that each category is totally independent; however, while memorization is unlikely to be used for a communicative purpose, some communication strategies might be used for a learning purpose. For example, an 'appeal for assistance' may well act as a learning strategy as well as a communication strategy. Tarone (1981) proposed a clear set of criteria for communication strategies and illustrated a number of such strategies which she observed in conversations with non-native speakers of English. Her criteria were:

1. speaker's communicative intent
2. speaker's belief that the means of expression are not available to one or other or both of the participants
3. speaker's choice – either avoid the meaning or use alternative means of expression.

Tarone's definition, involving intent, belief, and choice, put communication strategies firmly into the area of processing which one might legitimately expect to be available for conscious attention ('heeded processes' in Ericson and Simon's (1987) terms) and therefore potentially reportable by the user. Another important feature of this definition was the interactive nature of all three components – they are not merely private mental operations. Tarone suggests that learning strategies and perception strategies do not have this interactive nature – though the argument is less clear for perception strategies than for learning, since perception might be held to be partially dependent on beliefs about what the interlocutor intends to mean. Tarone (1977) listed a number of fairly broad categories of communication strategy which have been investigated by herself and other authors subsequently:

Paraphrase

Approximation – use of a single target-language (TL) vocabulary item or structure, which the learner knows is not correct, but which shares enough semantic features in common with the desired item to satisfy the speaker (e.g. *pipe* for *waterpipe*)

Word coinage – the learner makes up a new word in order to communicate a desired object (e.g. *airball* for *balloon*)

Circumlocution – the learner describes the characteristics or elements of the objects or action instead of using the appropriate TL item or structure (*She is, uh, smoking something, I don't know what's its name. That's uh, Persian, and we use in Turkey, a lot of*)

Borrowing

Literal translation – the learner translates word for word from the native language (e.g. *He invites him to drink* for *They toast one another*)

Language switch – the learner uses the native-language (NL) term without bothering to translate (e.g. *balon* for *balloon, tertil* for *caterpillar*)

Appeal for assistance – the learner asks for the correct term (e.g. *What is this?, What called?*)

Mime – the learner uses non-verbal strategies in place of a lexical item or action (e.g. clapping one's hands to illustrate applause)

Avoidance

Topic avoidance – the learner simply tries not to talk about concepts for which the TL item or structure is not known

Message abandonment – the learner begins to talk about a concept but is unable to continue and stops in mid-utterance.

Tarone quotes several studies on these phenomena, including an important unpublished study by Aono and Hillis (1979, quoted by Tarone, 1981). Aono and Hillis had recorded Aono's conversations with native speakers, then annotated transcriptions of these recordings with what

Aono remembered he had been thinking about while talking. This technique of 'stimulated recall' revealed evidence for many of the communication strategies mentioned by Tarone. Moreover, it showed that certain stretches of talk were in some sense 'rehearsed': the speaker had used them before in other conversations. The use of rehearsed sequences could be termed a 'production strategy' because it leads to fluency and presumably confidence, and does not imply Tarone's second criterion for a communication strategy: the speaker believed that the means of expression were available. However, the down-side of this use of rehearsed sequences was that they were fragile in the sense that, if interrupted, the speaker had little idea how to respond or continue, and in some cases the only reaction to interruption was repetition. Aono and Hillis also anticipated Cohen and Aphek's point that strategy use was determined in part by other circumstances and features – in the case of their subject by the learner's perception of the listener's interest, degrees of sympathy, or state of relaxation.

Faerch and Kasper (1983b) developed a model of strategy use at a higher level of generality which incorporated some important claims about how learners operate when attempting to accomplish conversations in foreign languages. The model was developed in an attempt to account for the behaviour of learners in two large-scale investigations of learner language conducted at Copenhagen, Denmark (the Project in Foreign Language Pedagogy (PIF), Department of English, University of Copenhagen) and Bochum, Germany (communicative competence as a feasible learning objective). In the PIF project, 130 face-to-face conversations were recorded between Danish learners of English at various educational levels and English native speakers; in the Bochum project, 48 face-to-face conversations were recorded between German first-year university students and English native speakers doing role-plays.

Faerch and Kasper divide the strategies into three very general kinds:

Formal reduction strategies: as when a language item which the learner has at his/her disposal is avoided, for example in order to avoid an anticipated error, or to increase fluency

Functional reduction strategies: as when certain normally required elements of speech acts like politeness formulae or apologies are omitted

Achievement strategies: these refer to most of the phenomena labelled by Tarone 'communication strategies' that are elaborative, which means that they do not involve reduction or avoidance but are devoted to compensation for perceived deficiencies:
  (*a*) code-switching
  (*b*) interlingual transfer
  (*c*) inter/intralingual transfer
  (*d*) interlanguage: generalization, paraphrase, word coinage

(*e*) co-operation: metalinguistic communication and appeals for assistance

(*f*) non-linguistic: mime, gesture, etc.

Faerch and Kasper present a schematic account of the relationships
between the use of these kinds of strategy, the *planning* and *execution* of linguistic problem-solving, and the types of situation and behaviour involved.
These relationships are represented in the form of a flow chart, represent-
ing a number of decisions by the speaker about when and how to plan an
utterance, when and how to retrieve information needed, when to avoid
formal and functional problems, and when to adopt achievement strategies.
It sets out a logical 'tree' of decision-making and therefore represents the
problem of strategy use as a cognitive process; but it does not incorporate
the kind of detail about other determinants of successful strategy use, such
as proficiency, time pressure, and personal characteristics, that Cohen and
Aphek discovered were important. Clearly, a full model of strategy use
requires a qualitatively richer specification of the determinants than even
Faerch and Kasper's already quite complex model. Bialystok's criticism of
it has already been mentioned in Chapter 1.

Strategic competence and individual characteristics

A paper by Haastrup and Phillipson in the same collection (Faerch and
Kasper 1983*a*) addressed some of these issues, attempting to describe the
individuality of particular learners participating in the PIF project in terms
of their preferred strategy use. From observation of videotaped inter-
actions, they analysed the learners' language and drew up profiles of each
learner. These were based on four kinds of information:

1. the nature of the interview
2. the patterns of breakdowns in communication
3. the kinds of achievement strategy used
4. the problems of understanding and perception apparent.

They give several examples of learners' conversations with native speakers,
with comments indicating additional information from the visual record
like gestures and their decision about the particular strategy being used
(see Fig. 2.1).

Haastrup and Phillipson perform this kind of analysis for several individual learners and present a summary for eight learners in their sample,
in which the frequency of disruption of communication is indicated and
is then broken down across categories of achievement strategy which that
learner regularly uses. In this way, a profile of strategy use for each learner
is obtained (see Fig. 2.2).

(L = learner, NS = native speaker

Transcript	Comment	Strategies
L: I bring petrol	= I deliver paraffin	literal translation/ anglicizing
NS: mm	simulates comprehension	
L: here in the winter there are a lot to do [...]	an explanation of the need for such work	paraphrase
NS: do you fill people's cars?		
L: no er		
NS: no is it?		
L: to heat up a room you need petrol	gesture	paraphrase + NV
and it's in 'dunke' you know	= jerry can; gesture	borrowing + NV
NS: yeah it er I mean in containers		
L: yeah in containers		
NS: yeah		
L: and ten litres in each		
NS: oh and you take it to people's houses and pour it in		
L: yeah bring it		lit. translation

Fig. 2.1 (*Source*: Haastrup and Phillipson, 1983: 146)

This kind of analysis goes some way to pinning down the individuality of strategy use in conversation, but prompts many more interesting questions, some of which Haastrup and Phillipson raise and attempt to answer:

1. What is the relationship between frequency of communicative disruption and communicative success? One might imagine it is a simple inverse relationship: the more disruption, the less communication. Haastrup and Phillipson point out that this is not so: the native speakers sometimes provoke breakdowns by being incoherent themselves; they also may choose to change topic rather than pursue a difficult one. The learners may fail to use strategies successfully.

2. What is the balance between L1 and interlanguage-based strategic styles? Haastrup and Phillipson confess surprise at the frequency of L1-based strategies.

3. Are there styles of strategy use which characterize groups of learners? Haastrup and her co-worker suggest that there are as many styles as there are learners.

Learner number	communication disruptions	L1-based strategies			IL-based strategies				cooperative strategies	non-verbal strategies	retrieval strategies
		borrowing	anglicizing	literal translation	generalization	paraphrase	word coinage	restructuring			
1	11	X	X						P	X	
2	21	X	X	X		X			PR		
3	15		X			(X)					
4	16					X			P	X	
5	42			X				X		X	
6	26			X		(X)			P		
7	30		(X)					X	PR		
8	30	X		X			X		P	X	X

X = regular use of the strategy
(X) = occasional use of each of the strategies in the set, i.e., L1-based or IL-based
P = presence of a production problem
R = presence of a reception problem

Fig. 2.2 (*Source:* Haastrup and Phillipson, 1983: 153)

4. Can achievement strategies be evaluated on some continuum from least effective to most effective? These authors claim their results suggest they can: interlanguage-based strategies lead more surely to success than L1-based strategies.

There are some further questions which these authors do not attempt to answer, but which will recur in subsequent pages and chapters:

5. Does strategy use vary with educational history?
6. Can strategic competence be taught?
7. Can strategic competence be evaluated independently of language knowledge?
8. Can these questions be answered on the basis of only eight profiles? How many does one need?

Compensatory strategies and think-aloud enquiry

The (relatively) large-scale corpuses of interactional data collected by the PIF and Bochum projects allowed a number of very useful observations of strategies in action. What was not collected was any data on the participants' beliefs as to why they had behaved in the way they had in the situation of communication breakdown. Another project on compensatory strategies, this time in the Netherlands, was conducted by Poulisse, Bongaerts, and Kellerman (1987) to try to do exactly this. Poulisse and her colleagues were concerned to validate their conception of when compensatory strategies were being used, and what strategy was actually in use, by inviting their respondents to comment. They used four different elicitation procedures; a picture description task, an abstract figure-description task, a story-retelling task, and a 20-minute interview with a native speaker. Only one of these tasks, therefore, involved communication in an interactional setting, and all were conducted outside the normal classroom situation. There were three groups of learners of English at different stages of proficiency. To collect the learners' introspections, video recordings were made of each learner doing all the tasks. The learners reviewed the playback and had the freedom to stop the tape at any point and comment. Their comments were recorded. Occasionally the researchers stopped the tape, triggering a comment, and infrequently asked a question. They were very wary about questioning because of the obvious danger of suggesting interpretations to the learners. The learners reported their comments in Dutch, their native language. The following extract (Poulisse *et al.*, 1987; 221) neatly illustrates the kind of rich data produced by the method. It is from an interview in which an advanced student is talking about her father's garden:

s: 2 erm, there he erm 1 erm he teels
   1. s: *that's not correct either [laughs]*
      E: no, you knew didn't you?
      s: 'verbouwen' (= 'to grow'), yes I knew
      E: yes
s: 2 erm 3 o jee 3 boons?
   2. s: 'sla' (= 'lettuce')!, salad isn't it?
      E: and 'bonen' (= 'beans')?
      s: *uh, bones?*
      E: beans
      s: *oh yes, beans, oh how stupid [laughs]*
I: what, what are they?
s: uh 'bonen' (= 'beans')
I: what are they like?
s: 'bonen' erm, little green [draws a bean in the air] uh 2 yes
I: vegetables, ja?
s: yes vegetables
I: mm
s: and erm 1 salade
   3. s: [laughs], that's from French [laughs]

I: mm
s: 1 erm, also flowers, uh dahlias (Dutch pronunciation)
   4. E: is dahlias also English?
      s: *no!* 1 well I don't really know
      E: no okay but I just wanted to know whether you knew 1 it prob-
          ably is, because she understands you
      s: oh, well yes *but she knows some Dutch*

Comments 1 and 2 are spontaneous confirmation of the identification of
the compensatory strategy of using a native-language word, and of course
of the student's full knowledge that the word chosen was not English. For
Poulisse *et al.*, and in view of the earlier discussion of strategy use, this
indication that she knew it was the wrong word in the wrong language is
crucial to the identification of strategy use. In the commentary (2), she
acknowledges the lapse she has made by forgetting the English *beans*. In
the third commentary, she explains her English mistake on *salade* by
acknowledging borrowing from French and in (4) she confesses that her
use of the Dutch pronunciation of *Dahlia* is because she knew the interviewer knew some Dutch and would therefore understand, even though
she believed that it was not a word in English.

In another example Poulisse *et al.* (1987: 222) point out that introspection can also sharpen the interpretation of learner language in terms of
compensatory strategies. Another student had a problem with the English
expression *pleated skirt*:

s: if he had uh, skirts with, plies
   1. s: 'plooirok' (= 'pleated skirt') I didn't know either
      E: you did know 'plooien' (= 'pleats')?
      s: yes, and skirt, so, at least, plies is 'plooien' (= 'pleats'), isn't it?
          it's not? [laughs] oh that
      E: [laughs] pleats
      s: what is that?
      E: uh, pleats, are 'plooien'
      s: oh, mm

Clearly this student uses a strategy of circumlocution to make *skirts with
plies* out of the Dutch *plooirok*, but she is confident that *plies* is an adequate
translation of the first element of that compound noun. She chooses not to
risk an English compound noun – *plieskirt*, but the uncertainty is about the
form of the nominal, not the English word *plies*. In discussion with the
experimenter, her mistake becomes clear. In this example, the retrospective evidence allows a detailed description of what the strategy consisted of.

Poulisse and her co-workers also present a quantitative analysis of
how much extra information the retrospective report data give. Overall,
using retrospective data increased the number of compensatory strategies

identified in their sample from 269 by observational criteria alone to 446 using observation and retrospection – an increase of 65 per cent. A closer look at the figures reveals that, taking into account cases where retrospective evidence disconfirmed an identification of a compensatory strategy, and those cases where the retrospective evidence merely confirmed an identification by other methods, the use of retrospective reports very nearly doubled the number of clear cases of use of compensatory strategies (260 using observation plus 263 using retrospection = 563 cases in their sample). Tarone's belief that the suggestion by Aono and Hillis of using verbal report data, and Cohen's use of it in several earlier researches, received dramatic confirmation in Poulisse *et al.*'s quantitative analyses.

Speech acts

Finally we turn to a situation of talk in a foreign language where errors can have disastrous consequences when non-native speakers are interacting with native speakers, especially where cross-cultural contact is involved. This is the area of the accomplishment of various speech acts. In the real world, learners need to act pragmatically in order to survive linguistically, not simply learn to perform adequately to pass some standard in a classroom situation. Several pieces of work have analysed these situations of speech act use in terms of the strategies learners use to accomplish or negotiate them, and the points at which their performance either breaks down or contrasts with the ways in which native speakers would accomplish the task.

These studies vary considerably with respect to the kinds of data they have used to analyse the understanding and performance of speech acts. Kasper and Dahl (1991) review thirty-nine studies of speech acts in terms of their variability in social and linguistic aspects, and also the variability of the studies in terms of the different ways of collecting data. One can observe these activities 'in the real world'; one can elicit them in role-plays; one can ask people in questionnaires how they would behave if faced with a particular situation. There is a whole range of ways of eliciting or observing this kind of behaviour, and inevitably each has its own effect on accuracy and validity of the conclusions that can be drawn. People have looked at understanding indirect answers, perceptions of politeness, requests, apologies, complaints, suggestions, invitations, compliments, and others.

Using naturally occurring data – English phrases addressed to him by Japanese speakers of English while carrying out various activities – White (1993) noticed that, in many cases his interlocutors used the form of a request using *Please* where an English native speaker would have used language more appropriate to the act of invitation, or direction-giving, or confirmation of arrangement, that is, something specific to the actual speech act being negotiated. Thus, inappropriate realizations of speech acts can produce misunderstandings that may be tolerated where both parties are in agreement about what is really happening, but may give rise to unintended offence if either party is unclear. In White's experience, many of his non-native-speaker conversation partners reduced their signals for different kinds of speech act to the same word, *Please*.

Olshtain and Cohen (1989: 53) give a neat example introducing their work on the speech act of apologizing:

> One morning, Mrs G., a native speaker of English now living in Israel, was doing her daily shopping at the local supermarket. As she was pushing her shopping cart she unintentionally bumped into Mr Y., a native Israeli. Her natural reaction was to say, 'I'm sorry' (in Hebrew). Mr Y. turned to her and said 'Lady you could at least apologise'.

Although the exchange used fully grammatical forms in Hebrew, it obviously did not work as an example of real apologizing. The reason was that, to count as an apology in that situation in Hebrew, apparently the direct translation of *I'm sorry* is not strong enough: it needs appropriate intensifying (*I'm really sorry*). Olshtain and Cohen set out a five element 'speech act set' for this particular act. In the context of this chapter, the interest lies in the use of questionnaires to find out what people attempting to accomplish an apology find most helpful in being taught these elements. Olshtain and Cohen's five elements are:

1. an expression of apology (with performative – *I'm sorry* – and optional intensifier – *really*)
2. an explanation or account of the situation (*I was going too fast*)
3. an acknowledgement of responsibility (*It was my fault*)
4. an offer of repair (*Are you sure you're all right*)
5. a promise of forbearance (*I'll be more careful next time*).

From this it can easily be recognized that making an apology requires quite an orchestrated set of performatives in order to satisfy these demands. In their 1990 study, Olshtain and Cohen attempted to discover what pedagogic moves were best received by students attempting to master these complications. The results favoured teachers' explanations most, class discussion least. This could be because group discussion is likely to be rooted within the students' culture, whereas the teacher can bring the perspective of the other culture to bear on the problem.

Cohen and Olshtain (1992) used retrospective verbal reports from fifteen advanced English as a Foreign Language (EFL) students, eleven of whom were native Hebrew speakers and four bilinguals in Hebrew and another language (French, Spanish, Portuguese, Arabic). The learners of English were given six situations on cards and their task was to role-play the situation and then to answer questions about why and how they had chosen the form of response they had. The situations were quite varied:

- apologizing for being late to meet a friend
- apologizing for keeping a classmate's book overlong
- complaining about a neighbour's loud noise
- responding to a refusal
- requesting a lift
- requesting a phone token off a friend.

The respondents gave interesting information on their strategic approach to these role-plays which Cohen and Olshtain roughly categorized as follows:

- pre-planning – particularly about the lift situation
- the language of thought – some tried to 'think like natives'
- the search and retrieval of forms:
  perceived difficulty
  retrieval and use of English
  self-debate – as between 'get a ride' and 'give a lift'
  afterthoughts
  awareness of accuracy
  using a commonly heard term
  omission
  breakdown
- delivering a different thought
- lexical avoidance and simplification
- approximation.

This very recent study produced some rather messy data, as interactive data usually are. However, it is one of the few studies in this field of how people plan and accomplish (or fail to accomplish) important interactional tasks in a foreign language which has begun to ask about the processes of executing those tasks. It is evident that the processes of accomplishing real work in a foreign language are very complex and, just as was found with the use of compensatory strategies in minor communicational breakdown, ways of discovering what learners are paying attention to and how they fight their way through difficult interactional situations are sorely needed. With that, we shall be in a better position to be able to understand what is going on when people attempt these tasks, and therefore what the true nature of second-language production skill is.

Process data from learners on how they perform the tasks and on what they find useful in order to learn the required language elements can then complement other kinds of input in the development of viable teaching strategies and the introduction of innovative syllabuses.

Summary and conclusions

This chapter has introduced a number of important approaches to decision-making by language learners in talk situations. The early work focused on the accomplishment of simple classroom exercises, but revealed surprising complications surrounding both success and failure. Later work explored strategies used in relatively free conversational situations, in which the need for keeping open the channel of communication and the two-way flow of talk exerts a pressure to compensate for actual or anticipated breakdowns. Learners develop a range of strategies for this situation, use of which depends on sophisticated evaluation of the possible breakdown, the interlocutor, and their own linguistic resources. Finally, work on strategies for accomplishing speech acts in a foreign language was introduced, leading to pedagogic implications for teaching those difficult interactional tasks such as requesting, apologizing, or refusing.

3

Receiving and understanding language: reading and listening

Introduction

Both reading and listening are uses of language for which even the word 'activity' is a metaphor. A person engaged in either may react, but need not; may show physical signs of following a track through time such as movements of the eye or head, but need not; may attempt to treat the source of the language as a live person and question or interrupt, but need not. This simple fact presents the biggest challenge both to the psychologist wishing to analyse the nature of these activities and to the teacher whose goal is to help a learner perform them as efficiently and deeply as possible. There is, however, a long tradition of belief that these so-called receptive skills are indeed activities and as such are both analysable and teachable, going back in this century to Huey (1968 [1908]) and Thorndyke (1917) at least. Reading and listening in a second or foreign language present the same problem to both analyst and teacher, with the added complication of variability in knowledge of the language. In this chapter we shall first look at a number of important issues in researching and teaching reading to non-native speakers, then explore the analytic research in both reading and listening, and finally attempt to draw some conclusions about the nature of these activities from the point of view of the participants' introspections.

Problems in reading and listening comprehension

Reading and listening

In many ways, reading and listening comprehension problems are very similar and so can be treated together. This is not always the case, of course, and the differences stem from two obvious facts. First, listening involves attention to a continuous stream of speech which is not under the timing control of the listener (the speaker decides how fast to speak), and second, many (but not all) listening activities involve active participation in conversation, with the need for coherent response from the listener. Third, of course, the medium of phonology is very different to the medium of writing. In both, on the other hand, larger units than individual sounds or characters have to be identified, sense relations evaluated, meanings extracted using knowledge of the language and knowledge of the world and the topic to constrain the possibilities, and a representation of the author's or speaker's meaning constructed. However, caution is required, and in what follows most of the text is about reading comprehension; what may be generalized to listening comprehension is a matter for discussion and empirical demonstration, other than the few specific studies of listening strategies to be discussed.

Skill, skills, or strategies

It is not difficult to argue that reading itself is a skill within the terms discussed in Chapter 1: in both L1 and L2 there are recognizable individual differences of speed, accuracy, smooth performance, sensitivity to feedback and confirmation, and success. It is more difficult to argue that there are reliably identifiable subskills or component skills, although it is often asserted. Nuttall (1982), for example, uses the idea of component skill to lay out a whole range of linguistic problems at word level and text level which a successful reader has to solve, with many sensible ideas for exercises to practise solving the problems. Each component skill is, however, the solution to a linguistic, metalinguistic, discourse, or pragmatic problem: skills are thereby defined only in terms of the task presented, not in terms of the mental behaviour of the reader. Several taxonomies of skills underlying reading have been proposed, such as Barrett's (1968, cited in Williams and Moran, 1989):

1. literal comprehension
2. reorganization of ideas in the text
3. inferential ability
4. evaluation
5. appreciation.

It happens that a number of empirical attempts have been made to isolate reading subskills, in this other, more psychological sense, but without much success. Williams and Moran (1989) cite Rosenshine (1980: 223): 'At this point, there is simply no clear evidence to support the naming of discrete skills in reading comprehension.' Lunzer's work with primary-school children in Britain (Lunzer and Gardner, 1979) points in the same direction. This failure to validate a set of skilled operations which combine to form skilled reading behaviour may mean that reading cannot in fact easily be broken down into its component skills by analysis of comprehension question answers, and that other approaches are needed.

For this reason, this chapter will follow a number of other authors in referring to reading *skill*, but discussing more local components as *strategies*.

Top-down or bottom-up

Any analysis of the task facing the non-native reader has to recognize that there are many aspects to the problem. For example:

- identification of word meaning
- recognition of grammatical cues
- recognition of print and orthographic cues
- use of contextual information
- use of background knowledge
- discrimination of author's intention
- discrimination of main and supporting points
- reconstruction of the argument
- recognition of the type of text.

All of these require both recognition of features of the text and appropriate interpretation, using knowledge brought to the task by the reader. A very broad distinction is commonly made between these two kinds of activity:

bottom-up, or text-driven, processes

v.

top-down, or concept-driven, processes.

Eskey (1988: 98) has argued persuasively for an interactive model, in which both these kinds of processing complement each other, and in which reading by less than proficient non-native speakers is represented by a relatively strong bias towards text-driven or bottom-up processes:

> Fluent reading entails both skilful decoding and relating the information so obtained to the reader's prior knowledge of the world. Thus the fluent reader is characterized by *both* skill at rapid, context-free word and phrase recognition, and, at higher cognitive levels, the skilful use of appropriate comprehension strategies. For the proper interpretation of texts the latter skills are crucial, but such lower-level skills as the rapid and accurate identification of lexical and grammatical forms are not merely obstacles to be cleared on the way to higher-level 'guessing game' strategies, but skills to be mastered as a necessary means of taking much of the guess-work out of reading comprehension. An interactive model of reading provides the most convincing account of this reciprocal perceptual/cognitive process.

Eskey is arguing essentially for a balanced view of two trends in reading research and exercise design which have evolved in the last few years. One, perhaps inherited from earlier psycholinguistic theorizing, emphasizes the use of language-specific knowledge to decode language elements: recognition of syntactic structure, lexical cohesion, word meaning, punctuation, morphology, etc. The other, also deriving in part from psychology, emphasizes the use of pre-existing knowledge of text structures and content to enable prediction and anticipation of events and meanings, and of inference of meaning from wider contexts. This approach is often referred to as *schema-theoretic*, following Carrell (1984) and Carrell and Eisterhold (1983). The first trend explored the bottom-up processes; the second trend investigated top-down processes. Eskey is, of course, arguing that a second-language reader needs skill at both kinds of processing in order to be a successful reader.

An interesting debate ensues when one considers Cloze passages. Good primary readers, as was shown by Neville and Pugh (1976–7), can use the information present on either side of a gap in the text; poor readers fail to. The obvious implication is that good readers can use some kind of problem-solving capacity to infer the meaning of the missing element or, perhaps, more cautiously, to arrive at an interpretation of the degraded phrase which is consistent with what they have so far read. In the case of Cloze passages, this indicates an active use of context, and therefore a kind of top-down process. The debate is about whether they actually behave in this way with complete texts. Where all the language cues are present, what is required is recognition of the significance of the written symbols (a bottom-up skill), which is a different matter from inferring the meaning of an absent symbol. Good L1 readers have little trouble in automatic word recognition; poor L2 readers have very great trouble in this area. Eskey's interesting point is that emphasizing top-down inference strategies for L2 learners of reading may be suggesting using one kind of strategy to compensate for failure of another kind, the bottom-up, in a situation where the L1 norm is bottom-up. L2 instruction based on such a principle may be encouraging an unnatural, compensatory way of processing a text rather than re-establishing the natural L1 process in the L2.

The evidence on this point is somewhat conflicting. In many situations, students find great difficulty in using cues in reading texts which indicate cohesion and the organization of ideas in the passage (Hooshmand, 1984, with Iranian students). Background knowledge of the content and topic of a passage helps students overcome linguistic difficulties in the text (Alvarez de Galicia, 1989, with Mexican students), but also leads to various kinds of error of comprehension where background knowledge of the topic or content is at variance with what the text actually says (Machado, 1985, with Brazilian students). However, activities designed to encourage schema-based processes are not necessarily successful. Youssef (1988) could not establish any differences in the reading performance of his Egyptian high-school students given reading-skill instruction of various types and 'traditional teaching' (presumably structure-based). Furry (1990) found that practice in decoding and making inferences was more important than a discussion of the topic of a reading passage in either the foreign language (French) or the native language (English). On the other hand, Kern (1988, with learners of French) claims that learners benefited more from instruction in strategies for handling discourse-level meaning than for dealing with word-level problems, and that low-level readers made the most gains. These pieces of research show a rather confused picture: foreign-language reading performance clearly requires accurate recognition of the linguistic cues in the passage and high-level processing of the meaning; but when this goes wrong, it is not clear if it is usually due to:

- failure of decoding skills
- use of inappropriate strategies
- failure of synthesizing skills
- failure of powers of inference from meaning to particular unknown words
- allowing preconceptions of meaning to override actual linguistic cues.

Since empirical discrimination between these kinds of failure is hard to come by using traditional comprehension tests and statistical treatments (Williams and Moran even doubt that a division into language and reasoning skills is defensible!), it is probable that the only way to elucidate these processes further is to use qualitative methods of gathering and interpretation of process data.

Language or reading?

Since it is possible to speak a language as a native without being able to read it, it is conventional to argue that reading is a skill of language use that is additional to, and to a certain extent separate from, language proficiency itself. (That is not, of course, to argue that being an illiterate native speaker is not a disadvantage for a citizen of a literate culture, or that illiteracy does not entail massive deprivation of cultural contact and sources of employment.)

Learning to read in a second language can therefore be seen as a dual problem of acquiring sufficient knowledge of the language itself and learning to use the reading skills present for the L1 in the L2. Alderson (1984) asked the simple question: is it a reading problem or a language problem? Poor second-language reading performance might be due to either a low level of language knowledge or a low level of reading skill for the L2.

Assuming, for the moment, that other factors such as motivation and interest are equal (an entirely indefensible assumption), the question may be put in a little more detail as follows. Is poor second language reading performance a reflection of:

(*a*)   a lack of L2 knowledge
(*b*)   low level of reading skill in L1
(*c*)   inadequate transfer of reading skill from L1
(*d*)   inappropriate reading skills for the particular L2?

The implication of (*a*) is either a correlation between L2 reading proficiency and a scale of L2 knowledge, or a cut-off point or threshold below which there is not sufficient basis of L2 knowledge for reading to be possible, and above which it is possible. Since the nature of L2 proficiency is highly complex and unlikely to be measurable on a single sliding scale – despite the language testers' penchant for global scales going from 'non-user' through 'modest' to 'expert' or 'beginner' through 'intermediate' to 'advanced' – the threshold idea is the more amenable to empirical research. It is exactly this idea that led Clarke (1979: 206) to propose that where students' knowledge of the language fell below a certain level, that lack 'short-circuited' the reading proficiency:

> apparently, limited control over the language 'short-circuits' the good reader's system causing him to resort to poor reading strategies when confronted with a difficult or confusing task in the second language.

Clarke's work was based on Cloze passage completion and on miscue analysis of oral errors by learners reading a passage aloud in Spanish (L1) and English (L2).

(*b*) implies that, given equal L2 proficiency, L2 reading performance would correlate with L1 reading levels: in other words, poor readers in their native language would become poor readers in their second language, and good in the one, good in the other. One difficulty with this argument is obviously that people have reasons for reading in the two languages, and often different reasons. That is why it is indefensible to assume no influence from motivation. Poor L1 readers may wish to develop greater reading performance in their L2 because that is the road to better employment through study or a period abroad. There does not seem to be any strong evidence which would deny that possibility. Another difficulty is that it is possible to identify individuals who fit into each of the four logical possibilities (see Table 3.1).

However, Monteiro (1992) did just that in her study of Brazilian technical high-school students, and performed a six-way comparison.

Table 3.1

	Good L1	Poor L1
Good L2	1	2
Poor L2	3	4

(*c*) is difficult to measure, but represents a frequent belief among teachers. Sometimes, students who apparently read reasonably well in L1 fail to extract meaning from L2 texts adequately and behave as if they cannot use the usual reading activities in an L2. Cooper's (1984) study of university students who had attended English-medium or Malay-medium schools provides a piece of empirical support for this idea: both the 'practised' (English medium) and the 'unpractised' (Malay medium) English readers scored equally well on a reading text in Malay using an academic style similar to English, but the unpractised readers performed markedly worse on many word- and sentence-level linguistic variables when reading in English (although both groups were, curiously, weak on syntactic knowledge).

(*d*) is usually discounted as a full explanation because it is manifest that many reading processes are universal, or have universal aspects; reading in every language requires word recognition, syntactic interpretation, assignment of meaning, interpretation of the message. But there are also language-specific reading skills: consider only the difference between word recognition in alphabetic writing and word recognition in Chinese or Japanese characters. For a person learning to read English, therefore, there are a number of things to learn about written English and how to decode it that they cannot bring from their mature L1 reading skills, because the decoding problem is different.

There have been a few recent and well-controlled attempts to answer Alderson's question. In Holland, Haquebord (1989; in Dutch, presented in English by Bossers, 1991) performed a longitudinal investigation of ethnic Turkish children enrolled in normal Dutch schools. Her results showed that, at the time of first testing (at an average age of 13.9 years and experience for the majority of the children of six years' full-time Dutch schooling), both knowledge of Dutch vocabulary and reading ability in Turkish were important, with the balance in favour of Dutch vocabulary knowledge. Two and a half years later, however, both these variables had reduced dramatically in importance. The suggested explanations for the change over time were that the Turkish children were losing their original ability to read in Turkish, as it was no longer an active study language; and that they were simultaneously behaving much more like native Dutch readers, because the relationship between reading and native vocabulary scores usually weakens in the same way as reading becomes more proficient. Thus, by the time these children were coming to the end of compulsory schooling, the differences between them in terms of reading Dutch had rather little to do with their original first-language reading level, or with simple measures of their knowledge of Dutch. Unfortunately, Haquebord does not report what other traits were related to their reading proficiency, such as academic success or intelligence. However, these intriguing explanations themselves need validating. This illustrates how easily a controlled study using a relatively large number of subjects can produce new questions rather than merely answer the original one.

In the United States, Carrell (1991) attempted to answer the question in another large-scale controlled study. She gave tests of L1 and L2 reading ability to a group of American college students studying Spanish and a group of Spanish speakers studying in an American college. Her results indicated that both knowledge of the foreign language and reading ability in the first language are important and contribute independently to the scores on the reading comprehension tasks. However, here again a surprising twist to the picture emerged: Spanish reading ability was more important than knowledge of English for the Spanish native speakers, but knowledge of Spanish was more important than native English reading ability for the native English learners of Spanish. Carrell suggests two possible explanations for this slightly bizarre outcome, both of which highlight the extreme difficulty of designing adequately controlled large-scale studies to answer seemingly simple questions. The first possibility is that she was dealing with two different kinds of second language user: speakers of English as a *second* language and speakers of Spanish as a *foreign* language, both operating within the predominantly English-oriented American college culture. Thus, cultural context of language use needs to be counterbalanced in a large-scale design. The second possibility is that differences in second-language proficiency were not random across the two groups but biased the results in some way. If, for example, the learners of Spanish were on balance worse at Spanish than the learners of English were at English, then one might expect (on Clarke's short-circuit hypothesis – see p. 39) that they would not be able to bring their native reading ability to bear on the texts as well as the other group. However, general L2 proficiency was not measured by Carrell in this study.

Bossers (1991) reports a highly controlled experiment conducted on Turkish learners of Dutch as a second language, in which reading comprehension, L1 reading skill, and L2 knowledge were assessed objectively. Bossers found that both L1 reading skill and L2 knowledge, as is to be expected, contributed to the differences in reading comprehension scores on the various tasks used. Moreover, in line with Carrell's main finding, level of knowledge of Dutch grammar and vocabulary was massively more important than level of reading skill in Turkish. However, Bossers found (1991: 56) that first-language reading skill came into play as an important factor for the 30 per cent most highly skilled second-language readers: 'The picture indicates, in other words, that knowledge of the target language plays a dominant role initially, and that L1 reading becomes a prominent factor at a more advanced level.'

This is strong support for the threshold hypothesis. Two very intriguing questions arise out of such a finding. First, to use it in a practical situation, one would want to know what the threshold looked like:

- What particular mix of second-language knowledge constitutes such a threshold?
- How does such a threshold relate to other aspects of language behaviour?
- Are there certain crucial language elements that have to be mastered?
- Does it bear any relation at all to any published syllabus thresholds, such as the Council of Europe's T-level?

Second, if passing the threshold enables a learner to use his good L1 reading skills in the new language, what does it do for the poor L1 reader – does it have a parallel enabling function for the development of new L2 reading skills? These questions still await answers.

Cultural meanings

A constant difficulty posed by learning to read in a second language is that L2 texts are usually written within the cultural assumptions of the speakers of that language, not within those of the readers' first language. 'Usually', because there is often one category of reading text exempted: that of classroom language-teaching materials written in the country of the users. However, as soon as a move is felt necessary towards authenticity of reading materials, even this exception disappears. In terms of the previous discussion of top-down and bottom-up processes, the problem of cultural differences is a slightly difficult one. Knowledge of cultural values, customs, and assumptions is clearly a kind of 'background knowledge' and, as such, is knowledge that the reader may or may not bring to the task of interpreting the text in a top-down fashion; but often the problem lies in recognizing the cultural significance of particular words, and belongs therefore to the domain of bottom-up processing, at least for the culturally fluent. Steffensen (1987) reviews a number of studies, and Steffensen and Joag-Dev (1984) have demonstrated dramatically how people from outside a culture may completely misunderstand a reported event because their own cultural connotations of colour are quite different. Steffensen and Joag-Dev found that North Americans and Indians failed to identify the activity of a wedding being reported in a text because each assumed the significance of white and black was the same as in their own culture, whereas in fact they are quite different.

Pritchard (1990), using texts about funerals in the United States and in a Pacific island culture, Palau, investigated strategy use by members of each culture reading culturally familiar and unfamiliar funeral practices in their own languages. He found that the Americans and the Palauans tended to use a somewhat different combination of strategies, whichever passage they were reading, so there was a strong cultural background effect on reading style. There was also a marked difference in all the subjects' behaviour reading the culturally familiar and unfamiliar texts – in particular, the search for connections within and across sentences. Reading the unfamiliar passage, compared to the familiar, there was significantly greater use of within-sentence connections, and dramatically less use of between-sentence connections. Pritchard interpreted this, on the basis of both counting the strategy use and analysing the think-aloud protocols qualitatively, to mean that readers tend to rely more on within-sentence clues, and turn away from more global links across the passage as a whole, when faced with the recognition of incomprehension. Even here, however, there was a cultural difference, as the American readers were more likely than the Palauans to persevere with the search for global meaning. Pritchard's research highlights the double problem that readers approach material from different cultures *both* with their own, culturally selected, reading strategy behaviour, *and* without crucial background information about the content itself. It is important to remember that his study shows this with readers reading in their own language, without the additional complication of L2 proficiency levels.

The 'cultural problem' in learning to read in a second language has a number of aspects. First, it is normal to think of it in a purely negative way: lack of cultural information makes the task more difficult; it is difficult to see how it could be facilitative. Second, most learners do not want to have to master massive amounts of cultural information about the society or societies where the language is spoken, and yet they need that information to avoid incomprehension. As yet there is little or no research on what learners do about this problem, how they recognize it, or least of all solve it.

Strategies in reading

Up to this point we have considered a number of current problems in L2 reading, looking at a range of different kinds of measure and reading activity. In line with the general theme of this book, we now turn to studies specifically focused on reading strategies of readers of different proficiency and ability levels in L2.

Early work

One of the earliest pieces of research on individual learners' reading strategies was conducted by Hosenfeld (1984). She attempted to identify what good readers seemed to be doing that poor readers were not, using an interview procedure in which she asked the learners (in their native language) what they were thinking about while they attempted to comprehend the texts. This research, then, used think-aloud protocols of a kind, in a case-study format. Hosenfeld then attempted to train poor readers in some of the word-attack strategies characteristic of the good readers in a further one-to-one interview session.

The successful readers used the following kinds of strategy, according to Hosenfeld's protocols (1984: 233–4):

- keep the meaning of the passage in mind
- read in broad phrases
- skip inessential words
- guess from context the meaning of unknown words
- have a good self-concept as a reader
- identify the grammatical category of words
- demonstrate sensitivity to a different word order
- examine illustrations
- read the title and make inferences from it
- use orthographic information (e.g. capitalization)
- refer to the side gloss
- use the glossary as a last resort
- look up words correctly
- continue if unsuccessful at decoding a word or phrase
- recognize cognates
- use their knowledge of the world
- follow through with a proposed solution to a problem
- evaluate their guesses

In her case-studies of unsuccessful readers, Hosenfeld used two sessions, an exploratory one and a remedial one. This is an extract from the exploratory session with Ricky, a ninth-grade poor reader of Spanish as a foreign language (Hosenfeld, 1984: 237–8):

Excerpt from: Los pueblos hispanoamericanos
   La vida diaria (daily) de un pueblo es tranquila, casi monótona. Nadie tiene prisa (Nobody is in a hurry). Los hombres se levantan temprano y van al trabajo. Muchos cultivan la tierra (land); algunos trabajan en las minas o en las pequeñas industrias del pueblo.
   Mientras los hombres están trabajando, las mujeres se quedan en casa cuidando de los niños y preparando las comidas.
   Los domingos por la mañana se oyen las campanas de la iglesia llamando a la gente a la misa.

A Translation of the Text: Spanish American Towns
   The daily life of a town is tranquil, almost monotonous. No one is in a hurry. The men get up early and go to work. Many cultivate the land; some work in the mines or small industries of the town.
   While the men are working, the women remain at home caring for the children and preparing the meals.

On Sunday mornings the church bells can be heard calling the people to mass.

R: (He reads aloud one sentence) The daily life ... of the town is tranquil ... tranquil ... *casi montana* ... *casi* (He turns to the glossary.) almost ... *montana* (He repeats the word, spells it out, and then returns to the text.) The daily life of the town is tranquil ... always ... *manotano* ... (He turns to the glossary.) monotonous (He turns back to the text.) The daily life of the town is tranquil ... and always monotonous. *Nadie tiene* ... Nobody is in a hurry. The men ... *se levanta* (He turns to the glossary, repeats *levanta*, and spells out the first letters as he scans the columns.) to get up (He turns back to the text.) The men ... get up ... early and go ... *el trabajo* (He turns to the glossary, repeats *trabajo*, and spells out the first letters.) to work (He turns back to the text.) The men get up early and go to work. Many cultivate ... the land ... *algunos trabajan* (He turns to the glossary, repeating the word *algunos*.) I think it means many ... any (He turns back to the text.) Any ... Many work in the mines ... or in ... the little industries of the town. *Mientras los hombres* ... *mientras* (He turns to the glossary and scans the columns, spelling out *mien* many times.) While. (He turns back to the text.) While many men ... have to get up ... the women ... *quandan* (He turns to the glossary, repeating the letter q; turns back to the text, spelling out many times the first three letters of the word; turns back to the glossary, spelling out the beginning of the word.) remain (He turns back to the text.) While many men ... have to get up ... have to leave ... the women ... remain ... in the home taking care of the children ... and preparing ... the meals. *Los domingos* ... *domingos* (He turns to the glossary, repeating the word.) Sunday (He returns to the text.) The Sundays ... *por la mana* (He turns to the glossary, and then back to the text.) Sundays in the morning ... *se oyen* (He turns to the glossary.) hear (He turns back to the text.) you hear ... the *campanas* (He turns to the glossary.) bells (He turns back to the text.) You hear the bells of the church ... *llamando* (He turns to the glossary.) They don't have this word in the book.

H: What word?

R: *Llamando*

H: What would you do?

R: Well it seems to me that ... it sounds like ... somebody's calling something ... *ando* ... it ends with i/n/g ... let's see ... the bells *llamando* ... are ringing ... *a la gente* (He turns to the glossary.) people (He turns back to the text.) They are calling the people ... *a la mesa* ... It sounds like they're calling them to mass (He turns to the glossary, scans the columns, repeating the word *mesa*, and turns back to the text.) *Misa* (He spells out the word and turns to the glossary.) (Sigh) mass . . . yes (He turns back to the text.) The bells are calling the people to mass.

In this extract there is very little intervention by the researcher. In the remedial session, Hosenfeld gave some specific instruction on various aspects of decoding, concentrating mainly on word-attack strategies (p. 240):

Los pueblos hispanoamericanos
. . . En la plaza hay árboles y flores, una fuente en el centro y varios bancos. En la plaza se encuentran tiendas, cafés, restaurantes y otros edificios. El edificio más alto, más bello y más importante es siempre la iglesia del pueblo.

R: In the plaza there are something and flowers, *una* something in the center and various benches.
H: Let's look at the first word, *árboles*. What kind of word is it?
R: A noun.
H: Does it look like an English word that would be appropriate in the sentence?
R: No.
H: What do we often find with flowers in a plaza?
R: (Silence)
H: Something in the same category.
R: Trees.
H: Does the word 'trees' fit into the sentence?
R: Yes.
H: Let's look at the next word, *fuente*. What kind of word is it?
R: A noun.
H: Does it look like an English word that would be appropriate in the sentence?
R: No.
H: They're talking about a plaza where there are trees and flowers. There is something in the center of the plaza. What might we find in the centre of the plaza?
R: A fountain.
H: Okay. Let's go on to the next sentence.
R: In the plaza something, something, cafés, restaurants and other something.
H: What is *se encuentran*?
R: A verb.
H: Does it look like an English word?
R: Yes. Encounters.

H: Let's figure out *tiendas*. In the plaza are found something, cafés, restaurants and other something. In the plaza are found cafés and restaurants. What else do we find in a plaza?

R: (Silence)

H: In the plazas we have around here?

R: Stores.

H: Let's look at the last word in the sentence. What kind of word is *edificios?*

R: A noun. It doesn't seem to look like a word in English.

H: Think of the whole sentence. In the plaza are found stores, cafés, restaurants and other what?

R: (Silence)

H: Look at the word again.

R: If you put the words all together ... if there are restaurants and cafés, there would have to be other buildings along with them.

H: Okay. Let's go on to the next sentence.

Several features of these transcripts and Hosenfeld's method are worth noting.

(*a*) A large amount of effort is devoted to translation. Ricky's idea of comprehension is to render the Spanish text into his own language. Consequently, not knowing a word's literal meaning is a big stumbling-block.. Hosenfeld's suggested strategy of using a sequence of clues to promote inferencing from context – first general meaning of the phrase, then information about the word, then speculation about cognates – teaches him how to overcome this particular problem.

(*b*) The distinction between research and teaching clearly breaks down in this particular type of one-to-one activity. It is easily possible that had Ricky had this kind of attention before he would not have been a poor reader anyway.

(*c*) Hosenfeld's assumption, borne out in previous research by her, that good and poor readers do different things, adopt different strategies, contrasts interestingly with earlier work on first language readers by Olshavsky (1976–7). Olshavsky had also used a think-aloud protocol technique, but a different one. Her subjects were instructed to say what they were thinking about at particular points in the text, marked by red dots on the page. These dots appeared at the end of most clauses and sentences. Olshavsky extracted a set of ten rather broadly defined strategies from the think–aloud protocols. A reported activity was only called a strategy if it occurred at least five times in the data, thus satisfying the criterion of a strategy being a repeatedly used way of solving a problem. Olshavsky found that her subjects made use of all of the strategies, but that there was a marked trend for strategies to be used more often if the readers were interested in the material, more often by more proficient readers, and more often with abstract (more difficult) material. Thus, whereas with her L2 readers Hosenfeld found differences of quality – poor readers tend to do different things from good ones – Olshavsky's L1 readers differed in terms of frequency of strategy use. It is still a matter of speculation, which only more detailed research could resolve, as to whether this difference is characteristic of L1 and L2 language reading, reflecting the different behaviour of poor L2 readers due to the lack of transfer of reading skill. Moreover, these two pieces of research used very different designs, so differences in outcomes could easily be due to other design features than the contrast between first and second languages.

Interviews with student readers

In what might be described as a variant of Hosenfeld's technique, Aslanian (1985) asked students of English as a second language (ESL) in New York to give him the reasons for their choices on a kind of 'modified Cloze' stimulus. Following their reading of a short passage in which some words had been blanked out, students had to choose an appropriate filler from a list and then discuss their choices. In the ensuing interview, the researcher's questions reveal more than just bottom-up or top-down strategies. Here is one of Aslanian's examples (1985: 24–5):

> *Transcript 3*
> o: What is the word that you have chosen for question (1)?
> s: *Boats.*
> o: Why did you choose that?
> s: Because I figure it's talking about boats, you know. The path, engineers, the river.
> o: Why do you think the others are not correct?
> s: We are not talking about the wind, etc. They are talking about bridges. We are talking about traffic, so it's got to be *boats*.
> o: What about question 2?
> s: I picked *levels*. They are talking about . . . it's talking about how to build tall enough bridges.
> o: Could you read the sentence with your choice?
> s: 'The *levels* will be too high. To save money, engineers . . .' OK. The *cost* would be too high.
> o: What made you change your mind?
> s: OK, I changed my mind because to save money engineers build movable bridges. So we're talking about money. So it could be *cost*.
> o: Why do you think *levels* was not the correct answer?
> s: 'cause we are talking about the uneconomical, so it has to do with money.
> o: Now, tell me everything you understood from this passage.

s: I think this passage is about the economy with traffic in ... you see, they're trying to build boats but they feel boats are too expensive because of the economy, the traffic, I guess; they feel that because we have too many traffic, the boats are very important, you know. Because in the river traffic we need more boats.

o: What else?

s: It's saying that we need tall ships that could be economical. Like what's the use of having too many ships if you can just have a big tall ship and get everybody in there and no too many ships to take up traffic.

o: Is that what you get from the passage?

s: Yes.

o: What else?

s: The passage is mainly about that the bridge ... the boat should not be built too high level because of the bridge. It would be uneconomical to build another bridge. So to economize, we shouldn't build boats too high.

o: It there any word that you don't understand in this passage?

s: *Movable* bridge. I'm not sure about it ... I haven't seen one.

o: Let's go back to the beginning of the passage for a moment. Can you tell me what the first sentence means?

s: It's trying to say that bridges are built high for the water path and the flow like the waves would not interfere with the bridge.

o: Where does it say that?

s: It says bridges are built to allow continuous flow of highway and railway traffic across the water lying in their paths.

o: What does the word *essential* mean?

s: Like *expensive*.

o: What does the word *uneconomical* mean?

s: OK. Economical would be like inflation, things that are happening.

o: If something is uneconomical, how do you think it is?

s: It means no use.

o: Why is it no use building high bridges?

s: I think it's no use because they haven't had any trouble; you know, that the ships are going under the bridge. Maybe the level is OK. It's no use to bring it any higher.

o: Do you have any comments?

s: My other problem is that I just don't like to read.

Aslanian comments that this student, prima facie, sounds like a reasonably proficient student in English, far more so than Hosenfeld's Ricky in Spanish. However, there are a number of serious problems. There is a lot of talk, but little of it seems to be relevant or to make much sense. The transcript eventually reveals a number of key vocabulary items whose significance for the meaning of the passage as a whole is not appreciated, in particular the word *movable*. This student (in common, oddly, with one of the other two quoted by Aslanian) could not visualize a 'movable' bridge. Also, the transferred sense of *flow*, here used of traffic, is not recognized at first, being confused with the mention of water under the bridges. There is, in fact, very little evidence here of strategy use in Hosenfeld's or Olshavsky's sense. However, in Aslanian's approach, the student is responding to questions from the researcher, and the data is therefore restricted by those questions.

Questions as data

One could object to Aslanian's approach that he is elevating a normal teaching process – asking comprehension questions – to a research technique, and in so doing biases the data he obtained. But another way of using questions has been suggested in the reading-methodology literature – asking students to ask questions during their reading – and this has also been used as a research technique in L1 studies with interesting results. So far, no L2 study seems to have used the technique. Olson, Duffy, and Mack (1984) asked skilled L1 readers to formulate questions as they read stories sentence by sentence. They found that the number of questions asked by one group of readers was closely related to the amount of time spent by another group of silent readers reading the same sentences, but did not relate to their final recall of the text. The implication is clearly that as you read, you review and update the information you have obtained and which you need in order to construct an interpretation; question-asking reflects that information supply and demand. Thus a particular form of think-aloud protocol, question-asking, reveals details of the ongoing process of reading in both a qualitative and quantitative fashion. In Olson *et al.*'s study, final recall was more strongly connected with where the sentence came in the text (serial position) and the rated importance of the content. So, think-aloud protocols may have more to do with the process of reading than with the final product for native readers, just as they may have more to do with the process of learning to read for non-native readers.

Poor readers' strategies

In many ways, although a theory of reading in L2 has to specify how all readers perform, practical interest centres naturally on unsuccessful readers. A piece of research by Block (1986), using a think-aloud method similar to Olshavsky's, attempted to explore approaches to reading for educational purposes by a number of readers of low standard. A particularly interesting feature of her study was the inclusion of both non-native and native readers of the same educational level (college first-years who had failed a college reading-ability test). Block isolated a number of reading strategies employed by these readers.

General

1. anticipate content – 'I guess the story will be about how you go about talking to babies'
2. recognize text structure – 'This is an example of what baby talk is'
3. integrate information – 'Oh, this connects with the sentence just before'
4. question information in the text – 'Why is baby talk among adults usually limited to lovers?'
5. interpret the text – 'I think that's why some people are doing this thing'
6. use general knowledge and associations
7. comment on behaviour or process – 'I'm getting this feeling I always get when I read like I lost a word'
8. monitor comprehension – 'Now I see what it means'
9. correct behaviour – 'Now I read this part I understand . . . I misunderstood in a way'
10. react to text – 'I love little babies'

Local

11. paraphrase
12. reread
13. question meaning of clause or sentence
14. question meaning of a word
15. solve vocabulary problem – 'Straightforward grammar, means easy grammar'

Block gives an example of a subject's think-aloud protocol, coded for strategy use, which is reproduced here (1986: 493–4):

Text	Response
1. All of the world's languages, from English to Urdu, share one special kind of speech: baby talk.	It's baby talk. What's baby talk and Urdu?
2. Recent research has confirmed that in spite of the great differences among cultures and languages, the general properties of speech used with babies who are learning to talk remain the same.	Recent research has confirmed . . . that in spite of the great differences among cultures and languages the general practice of speech used with brothers who learning to talk remain the same . . . What's general practice of speech?
3. Baby talk sounds different from adult speech.	Baby talk sounds different from adult speech. Oh I see. They trying to point out the difference between baby talk sounds and adult speech.

Text	Response
4. When talking to 1- and 2-year olds, adults usually raise the pitch of their voices and adopt a 'sing-song' intonation, in which the voice rises and drops dramatically, often ending a sentence at a high point.	When talking to 1 and 2 year olds, adults usually raise the pitch of their voices and adopt a raising, a singing sound, in which the voice rises and drops dramatically, often ending a sentence at a high point ... The main point, how adult talk to babies, and the baby learn from, and the voice always higher and, you know, like a melody.
5. (Imagine the way you would say to a baby, 'Hi, Johnny. You're playing with your teddy, aren't you?')	Imagine the way you would say to a baby. 'Hi, Johnny, you're playing with your teddy, aren't you?' [Raises voice, imitates baby talk.] Cause adults always talk that way.
6. What is the point of these peculiarities?	What is the point of these peculiarities? What's the word, peculiarities? I don't know, I just go ahead and read.
7. Research has shown that babies prefer sounds in higher pitch ranges.	
8. Adults may quickly learn that they are more likely to get a smile or a satisfied gurgle from a baby when they raise their voices a bit.	Adults may quickly learn that they are more likely to get a smile or a ... What's this? Satisfied giggle from baby when they raise their voices. Oh now, it telling the reason why adult do this. It do this on purpose when they want a giggle or smile from their babies.
9. And the melodious rise and fall of the speech signal may hold the baby's attention – something that isn't easy to do.	And fall of the speech signal may hold baby's attention, something that isn't easy to do. Oh, now tell you baby talk also can hold attention. Sometimes when we listen to speech, you not hold your own's attention so easily so some people use approach in the other paragraph. Think, I think that's why some people doing this baby talk.

Several observations are prompted by this.

(a) A large amount of the reader's talk is reading the text aloud as if doing a miscue analysis task. This was true of this reader, and is indicative of a style of response. However, it was not characteristic of most of the readers in the study.

(b) The method of requiring response at the end of each sentence may well produce a response bias – in fact, it was reported by two of the readers to cause discomfort. But others felt they learned from it and actually seemed to feel liberated once they were able to attend their own processing.

(c) Misidentification of words leads to the use of strategies – 'properties' > 'practice' and 'babies' > 'brothers' in sentence 2.

(d) Several comments show perception of the argument structure.

Quite clearly, a number of these strategies are familiar from work we have already discussed. The distinction between general strategies and local strategies is echoed in Hosenfeld's 'meaning-line' and 'word-related' strategies, and in Olshavsky's 'word-level' and 'sentence-level'; 'paraphrase' and 'synonym' are close relations; 'personal identification' and Block's 'general knowledge and associations' are very close. A detailed comparison of the occurrence of strategy labels will be presented in a later section; most pieces of research identify some of the same strategies and add others, depending among other things on the data collection method, the particular subjects, and the type of text.

An interesting feature of Block's analysis is her recognition of two modes of response to the reading, and of two kinds of reader who are associated with these modes. Block talked about *extensive* and *reflexive* modes of response, borrowing the terms from studies of writing. Responding in extensive mode means remaining fairly closely tied to the text, whereas reflective responding means applying to the text with large amounts of personal comment, identification, and anecdote. Some students responded in extensive mode all the time, some mainly reflexive, and some mixed. Associated with these modes were two patterns of strategy use, 'Integrators' and 'Non-integrators'.

Integrators
- responded in extensive mode
- reacted to text structure
- monitored their understanding
- highlighted the main theme in their retellings

Non-integrators
- responded in reflexive mode
- reacted less to text structure
- made fewer attempts to connect
- reported more details and fewer main ideas in retelling

These patterns of strategy use were related to other measures of academic progress: the three Integrators produced higher grade point averages than the Non-integrators in their first semester.

These results are, of course, somewhat tantalizing. We do not know if Block's distinction is robust enough to hold up with a large number of readers. However, the distinction she draws reflects a genuine dimension of uncertainty in an unproficient reader: how to temper the flow of personal associations and reactions to elements of the text with appreciation of the argument and overall structure of the text, how to reconstruct the balance of the argument and supporting or contrasting detail in a text as the reader's version of the author's intended meaning. The association between being an Integrator and having a marginally higher grade point average – even with these substandard readers – points to the desirability of such a pattern of strategy use.

Metacognitive strategies

Hosenfeld's and Block's research looked at actual students in process of reading various texts. Their studies, therefore, have an authority derived from the immediacy of the activity, but their results are limited not only by the small numbers of readers involved but also by the actual text being read. Different texts provide different challenges which call for different solutions and therefore strategy use. Carrell (1989) decided to use a questionnaire approach to investigate a range of strategies. This approach frees the data from dependence on actual reading situations, but it does so by asking readers about their beliefs as to what they would do in hypothetical circumstances. Carrell was particularly interested in readers' strategies for organizing information processing: metacognitive strategies. She used the questionnaire to probe readers' perceptions of their strategies in silent reading of their first and second languages, and then asked what relationship might hold between these strategies and the participants' reading ability. The questions concerned four aspects of reading strategies (Carrell, 1989: 124, fig. 2):

1. *Confidence*
   6 statements related to various aspects of a reader's perceived ability to read in the language.
   e.g. 'When reading silently in Spanish, I am able to recognize the difference between main points and supporting details.'

2. *Repair*
   5 statements related to repair strategies a reader uses when comprehension fails.
   e.g. 'When reading silently in English, if I don't understand something, I keep on reading and hope for clarification further on.'

3. *Effective*
   17 statements related to reading strategies the reader feels make the reading effective: subcategorized into: sound–letter (3 statements); word-meaning (5 statements); text-gist (2 statements); background knowledge (2 statements); content details (2 statements); text organization (2 statements); sentence syntax (1 statement).

e.g. 'When reading silently in Spanish the things I do to read effectively are to focus on the organization of the text.'

4. *Difficulty*
   8 statements related to aspects of reading which make the reading difficult; subcategorized into: sound–letter (3 statements); word-meaning (1 statement); text gist (1 statement); text organization (1 statement); sentence syntax (1 statement).
   e.g. 'When reading silently in Spanish, things that make the reading difficult are the grammatical structures.

Carrell found that there was some difference between strategy perceptions associated with good L1 readers and those associated with good L2 readers. With the Spanish native speakers, the only significant effects were in the 'Effectivity' and 'Difficulty' sections: readers who strongly disagreed with doing 'local' things like sounding out parts of words, construing the syntax, and looking at content details came out as better readers. With the English native speakers, the only point that marked out the good readers was that they disagreed with the idea of looking at details of sound–letter relationships while reading.

The most remarkable feature of the data on reading in the native language was how few of the items on the questionnaire actually showed up as relevant overall for reading, suggesting that reading in one's first language is on a plane of automaticity which these questions about reading cannot tap into. With regard to reading in the second language, Carrell's data showed a consistent difference according to proficiency level. For the Spanish-speaking learners of English, operating in an English-speaking American culture, more global or top-down strategies were associated with L2 reading ability. For the English-speaking learners of Spanish operating in their home culture, more local or bottom-up strategies were associated with reading ability in the L2.

The Spanish-speaking group comprised 45 students, 8 at level 3 (intermediate), 20 at level 4 (advanced), and 17 enrolled in a university composition class; the English-speaking group comprised 75 students, 23 at level 3, 13 at level 4, and 39 at level 2. Clearly, the different proficiency profile of the two groups played a major part in the different kinds of reading strategies acknowledged by them. It would, however, have been instructive to have isolated groups of similar proficiency – say, the level 3 and 4 users of the two languages – and presented a breakdown of their strategy use, because this would have allowed a direct comparison of strategy use uncomplicated by gross differences of proficiency within the groups. Carrell herself points out that 'these meta-cognitive results are to be taken as suggestive rather than definitive' (1989: 128). However, these results provide confirmation for the idea that strategy use is related to language-proficiency level in general terms, and that the differences are of quality rather than quantity. Lower-proficiency readers tend to report more text-bound, local strategies than higher proficiency students, presumably reflecting the area of reading where their greatest problems lie.

Monteiro (1992) used Carrell's metacognitive questionnaire in a different way: as an interpretive device for analysing the strategy use reported in think-aloud protocols. Her subjects, students in Brazilian technical high schools, gave information while reading in both Portuguese and English in Olshavsky's protocol analysis method. Monteiro was thus able to obtain partial confirmation of Carrell's questionnaire-based findings in a process-oriented study. Monteiro concluded that language proficiency was the major factor in her results, both as regards the degree of comprehension and with respect to the patterns of strategy use adopted by the students.

Comparison of reading in L1 and L2

A theme which has already appeared, particularly in discussion of the work by Block and Carrell, is the comparison of strategy use when reading in L1 and in L2. A piece of research by Sarig (1987) investigated this question directly, using a think-aloud protocol method rather than the questionnaire method favoured by Carrell. Although Sarig's paper is entitled 'High level reading', her subjects were 17–18-year-old girls at the end of their school careers, rather than students grappling with degree-level material. They had Hebrew as L1 and English as their foreign language. Sarig found that, overall, the readers' use of strategies, and the relation between strategies used and actual success in comprehension, was highly similar in both languages. Moreover, her subjects' strategic choices correlated highly in each stage of reading, such as identifying the propositions in the text, identifying the main ideas, and synthesizing the actual message. Of course, this is entirely what one would expect on the threshold theory (see p. 39) of skill transfer, if these school-leavers' knowledge of English was indeed above the threshold level.

Sarig claims to have separated out which strategic moves contributed to success and which to failure (though her report is not explicit on how this was achieved). There is even a large measure of agreement between L1 and L2 use concerning those moves which promoted comprehension and those which did not. However, Sarig also found that individual readers differed within this global picture quite markedly, in particular in terms of the selection of strategies, rather than the total number of strategies used. This recalls Hosenfeld's original finding, and contrasts with Olshavsky's claim (which referred only to L1 readers). Sarig's results were original in the specification of combinations of moves that brought success and in those that ended in failure. She makes the point (1987: 118):

Moreover, readers use a majority of comprehension-promoting moves and still fail as a result of a few wrong moves or even a single wrong move. This does not turn them into poor readers. The same is true of readers who make more comprehension-deterring than comprehension-promoting moves and still perform the task successfully, thanks even to one smart move which outweighs the other comprehension deterring ones.

Reading strategies: a comparison

Perhaps the most useful aspect of Sarig's work is the classification of strategies, called by her 'moves', into four categories:

- technical aids moves
- clarification and simplification moves
- coherence-detecting moves
- monitoring moves.

In what follows, the strategies identified in the research discussed earlier will be brought together within these categories. These strategies or moves are those that have been identified by researchers interpreting the think-aloud data: they do not include the questions in the Carrell metacognitive questionnaire, which concern a different kind of data. There is, of course, no final certainty in equating similar-sounding strategies from different pieces of research; thus, whether Sarig's 'identifying the macroframe', Hosenfeld's 'keeping the meaning of the passage in mind', and Olshavsky's 'use of information about the story' are really the same strategy is impossible to decide: they bear a family resemblance.

1. *Technical aids*
   skimming
   scanning
   marking the text
   making a paragraph summary in the margin
   using glossary (Sarig, Hosenfeld)
   recognizing cognates (Hosenfeld)
   examining illustrations (Hosenfeld)
   using context to define a word (Olshavsky)

2. *Clarification and simplification*
   syntactic simplification (Sarig)
   producing synonyms and circumlocutions (Sarig, Block, Olshavsky)
   using paraphrase of rhetorical function (Sarig)
   paraphrase (Block)
   identifying grammatical category of words (Hosenfeld)

interpreting the text (Block)
using inference (Olshavsky)
addition of information (Olshavsky)

3. *Coherence detection*
identifying the macroframe (Sarig)
keeping the meaning of the passage in mind (Hosenfeld)
using information about the story (Olshavsky)
using general knowledge and associations (Block)
using knowledge of the world (Hosenfeld)
using background knowledge (Sarig)
identifying key information (Sarig)
anticipating content (Block)
hypothesizing (Olshavsky)
recognizing text structure (Block)
integrating information (Block)

4. *Monitoring*
consciously changing the plan (Sarig)
holding (Block)
deserting a hopeless utterance (Sarig)
varying the reading rate (Sarig)
rereading (Block, Olshavsky)
identifying misunderstanding (Sarig)
stating failure to understand a word or a clause (Olshavsky)
correcting mistakes (Sarig, Block)
skipping in a controlled fashion (Sarig, Hosenfeld)
self-directed dialogue (Sarig)
evaluating guesses (Hosenfeld)
following through with a solution to a problem (Hosenfeld)
questioning information in the text (Block)
commenting on behaviour (Block)
monitoring comprehension (Block)
reacting to text (Block)
questioning meaning of clause, sentence, or word (Block, Sarig, Hosenfeld)

Strategies in listening

Murphy (1985) and O'Malley, Chamot, and Küpper (1989) have attempted to glean introspective evidence from learners about their listening comprehension. While in many ways listening has a number of special problems, owing to the time pressure of attending to the stream of speech, it is instructive to compare the categories which learners use to talk about it with those used in reading comprehension. The parallels are in fact quite close. O'Malley *et al.* identified three particular groups of strategies – self-monitoring, elaboration by using background knowledge, and inferring the meaning of words and phrases from context. Moreover, they showed that the use of these strategy types differed according to a division of the students into effective and ineffective listeners. The more effective listeners used a more 'top-down' approach, recalling Carrell's work with readers; the less effective concentrated on a word-by-word approach, 'bottom-up'.

While this is perhaps in the expected direction, it is not entirely surprising from another point of view either, since the criterion for dividing the group into effective and ineffective listeners rather pre-empted the contrast drawn: one of the criteria was 'ability and willingness to guess at the meaning of unfamiliar words and phrases'. The other criteria related to attentiveness in class, ability to follow directions, ability and willingness to understand a difficult listening text, and appropriate conversational responses: in other words, their teachers' ratings of the students as participants in the classroom and general communicative proficiency, not some independent test of their listening skill.

Nevertheless, the students' think-aloud protocols are instructive. As usual, background knowledge is a mixed blessing. The 'effective' students used their own knowledge to help them elaborate the text and infer the meaning; but while providing an interpretation, it was often inaccurate (O'Malley *et al.*, 1989: 432):

> Text listened to: '... At that time, Germany owed a lot of money as a result of the Second World War. The British and American [car] experts thought they might take over the Volkswagen factory. By taking over the manufacture of Volkswagens, they thought Germany could pay back some of the money she owed.'

> Student response: 'On that bit I really did get lost ... like Germany in going to pay the United States. that the United States is ... and England owes it. Like ... ah! Now I understand. It was because of the Volkswagen. Since they are going to sell it over here, they make more money, and then with that money Volkswagen is going to pay back all that money they lost.'

'Ineffective' listeners spent their time working out words (p. 429):

> 'Well, first I listened to each word that she [the tape] was saying, I grasped it ... but not really all of them.'

However, there is an obvious contrast here with Block's poor readers, a majority of whom mixed up personal associations and background knowledge with the information from the text – the 'Non-integrators'. One could speculate that perhaps the time pressure in listening actually prevents this type of response. It would be worth pursuing in a properly controlled investigation.

Summary

At this point it is desirable to summarize what has been learned so far about comprehension processes from the point of view of reception strategies and learner introspection.

Are comprehension processes analysable in terms of strategies?

Quite clearly, yes. Although there are many aspects of reading and listening skill which are automatic and from this point of view ineluctable, there are also many facets which are revealed by the sensitive techniques of protocol analysis.

Do protocol analyses add significantly to the information from other kinds of data analysis?

Analysed carefully, the information gained from think-aloud protocols on students' awareness of how they approach the tasks increases our knowledge in at least two ways:

- elaboration of the details of the process
- highlighting individual differences

Do individual differences stand out?

The data described show quite considerable individual variation. Some of this correlates with measures of proficiency, indicating a link between strategy use and success, and some of it does not, indicating wide variation in individuals' approaches to similar problems and within individuals.

Are there characteristic patterns of strategy use or choice for different levels of skill?

In general, a common theme is that learners with a low level of skill use 'bottom-up' strategies and learners with a high level of skill use 'top-down' strategies. This is echoed also in the O'Malley listening study. However, one should be wary of inferring cause-and-effect relations. This general pattern may simply reflect general L2 proficiency. An L2 reader without a well-developed knowledge of the language is not in a position to use anything but word-attack and low-level parsing skills: encouraging them to use higher-level inferencing as recommended by Hosenfeld may be possible but may be dependent for its success on the teacher's guidance, as in her own examples.

Do reading and listening skills transfer from the first language?

For listening there are simply no data; for reading the picture is quite complicated. It seems that they do, but that it depends on some kind of 'threshold level' of L2 knowledge. However, specifying that threshold in terms of, say, syntactic structures or critical mass of vocabulary has not so far been possible. There is also the problem of situation of language use: the American work indicates a possible difference in terms of 'foreign' and 'second' language use (but, as we saw, it is confounded with proficiency level), and the Dutch work indicates a reduction of L1 influence during the immigrants' school career.

Do the protocols reveal more than reactions to the text?

The largest category of strategies (therefore the category with the widest variation, and possibly the category with the least well-defined nature) is 'monitoring'. L2 readers do a great deal to organize themselves as text-processors; a considerable amount of energy is devoted to this aim. Furthermore, these strategies also reveal many links with wider issues connected with being a learner, such as motivation to learn and interest in the vehicle of learning – the content of the text.

Are there implications for teaching practice and exercise design?

Undoubtedly yes, but, as we shall see in the chapters on learner training and classroom instruction, one has to be very careful in going straight from research to prescriptions for teaching. The explication of text-based strategies and the identification by Cohen et al. (1979), through student introspections, of various impediments to comprehension like 'heavy' syntax and 'semi-technical' vocabulary in ESP (English for special purposes) reading give some pointers. Several of the pieces of research attempted to pinpoint how teachers' guidance might help a student change from floundering novice to independent expert. However, no set of effective teaching procedures can be said to emerge from this exploration of student strategy use. If there is a practical message in what these students are telling us through the strategy data, it is that we should try to establish what our students actually do and learn to evaluate for them as individual learners whether they are acting in a way that will lead them to progress.

4

The writing process

Introduction

This chapter will explore the research into what second-language writers can tell us about their writing, their approaches to it, their feelings about it, what takes their attention while they write, and how they utilize feedback on what they have written. The chapter is organized around the following themes.

Writing in the first language

We begin with a brief look at the seminal studies of people writing in their native language.

Protocol analysis

The version of 'protocol analysis' used in writing studies will be discussed – a term we have already met in a slightly different guise in discussing reading, and which has been used in studies of both first- and second-language writing.

Criticisms of protocol analysis and process studies

Some of the criticisms of this technique and of the general theoretical orientation behind it need to be addressed, because it is by no means uncontroversial.

Process studies of writing in a second language

Moving on to people learning to write in a second language, we first attempt to see just what can be revealed in a general way about an individual's writing process when we ask them to comment on the writing as they are doing it.

Writing in two languages

Next, we look at case studies devoted to specific questions of writing in two languages. These questions are the influence of the first language and the similarities between writing strategies in the first language and the second.

Cultural factors

These questions lead naturally to a discussion of the influence of cultural factors on the production of text, given that in many cases people writing in a second language are operating in a cultural situation which differs from the one in which they would use their mother tongue.

Reviewing, revising, and editing

A vital component for the production of text is the need to revise and edit what you have written. The amount and the efficiency of these operations are clearly determined by your proficiency as a writer and also by the kind of writing that is demanded from you, and this is the next issue to be investigated.

An example of protocol analysis

In this section a short example of a 'think-aloud' protocol produced by an EFL student writing a free composition on a given topic will be presented and analysed to illustrate the kinds of insights to be gained from considering two sources of evidence: the written product and what the writer says while producing it.

Feedback

Finally we discuss the role of feedback from readers: in this context the readers are mainly but not only the teachers. There are two sides to this issue: how teachers formulate the feedback they give and how learners use that feedback once received. There are some surprising results in this area: feedback is the sting in the tail.

Investigations

Writing process studies in the first language

Perl (1980; 1981), who had already instigated something of a revolution in attitudes to writing in the liberal arts community in the United States with her study of the composing processes of under-prepared college students, drew on some of these results to present a view of writing which is opposed to the classical view of planning followed by writing followed by revising. Her view is of writing as a recursive process, a process in which the writer returns to various elements of the text already produced before going ahead to produce more text. She points out that recursive moves are not always a return to what has preceded the point of utterance; writers tend also to wander back to certain key words, as if contemplating them will produce some new element that will guide the next part of the text; and also writers return to less tangible guidelines for which she coined the term 'the felt sense'.

Perl also proposed a technique of investigation in which writers talk about their writing at the same time as they work on their text. Proponents of this technique of 'thinking aloud' distinguish it from introspection and self-report, which are notoriously unreliable ways of obtaining data; however, it has been heavily criticized, as we shall see. In a working paper outlining this technique, Perl put forward a set of coding categories and gave several examples of how they operated. The categories were divided into a set of major activities with a number of minor variations on each, indicated by sub- or superscripts. The protocol produced by the writer was transcribed on to a time grid, so that the amount of time devoted to each activity and the frequency and time course of changes of activity could be plotted. Using this technique, Perl investigated both experienced writers and under-achieving student writers.

Using the same generally mentalist approach as Perl, a cognitive psychologist, J. R. Hayes, and a composition teacher, L. Flower, developed a model of the writing process and attempted to use it to explain many puzzling features of the protocols obtained from writers (Flower and Hayes, 1980; 1981; Hayes and Flower, 1983). They also rejected the simple linear assumption that writers plan, then write, then revise, and more strongly rejected the approach to teaching writing that prescribed this linear plan for student writers. By contrast, they viewed the writer as being involved in a constant, ongoing problem-solving exercise, where at any moment different tensions have to be harmonized, different constraints satisfied. They gave this process the rather fanciful image of 'orchestration'. 'Writing is best understood as a set of distinctive thinking processes which writers orchestrate or organise during the act of composing' (1981: 366).

According to Hayes and Flower, writers still do plan and write and revise, naturally (their terms are 'planning', 'translating', and 'reviewing'). These are integral parts of the *writing process*. However, these basic activities are considered to be:

(*a*) *hierarchically structured*, because each consists of sub-processes: thus planning subsumes goal-setting and organizing; reviewing subsumes evaluating and revising.

(*b*) *independently organized,* in that each contributes to the writing process and may occur in any order with respect to the others: you can (and people do) write without planning, and review without writing. It also suggests you can review without planning, but this would be either meaningless or difficult to distinguish from planning anyway.

(*c*) *interacting* with two other important sources of information:

1. the *task environment,* which is made up of the rhetorical problem posed by the piece of writing (the topic and the audience) and by the text produced already, which severely constrains the writer's choices both on grounds of coherence, development of the argument, and avoidance of repetition, and in terms of lexical and grammatical decisions
2. the writer's *long-term memory,* in which is stored knowledge of the intended audience, the topic, and of plans for writing used or rejected before.

Interaction between these three complexes, *writing process, task environment,* and *long-term memory,* is thought of as constant and multidirectional. 'Part of the drama of writing is seeing how writers juggle and integrate the multiple constraints of their knowledge, their plans, and their text into the production of each new sentence' (Flower and Hayes, 1981: 371).

Criticisms of the process approach

However attractive these ideas on the psychology of writing may be, both the kind of theory they form and the kind of evidence which Flower and Hayes and Perl sought to test them against have been quite strongly criticized on methodological grounds. For instance, Cooper and Holzmann (1983) pointed out that Flower and Hayes seem to confuse the cognitive process, which is essentially unobservable, with the product of that process: thus giving unwarranted *factual* status to their *inferences* about how a particular piece of text was put together. Cooper and Holzmann argue that 'models of cognitive processes cannot, in principle, be valid as literal description' (1983: 285). This refers to the impossibility of using a model of an unobservable internal cognitive process as a description of an observable piece of behaviour. However, it does not rule out the possibility that a piece of observable behaviour might be caused by an unobservable cognitive process which the model captures. This raises the important question of how such models can be tested and validated. A further criticism they make of Flower and Hayes is that studies of talking aloud while writing do not test the model; rather, terms from the model are used as descriptive codings.

Cooper and Holzmann also argued that Flower and Hayes's model was under-specified: it did not make sufficiently fine discriminations, focusing in particular on the failure to define a goal in the writing process and distinguish it from a plan. More practically, they said 'it is, after all, rather an odd thing to talk about what you are thinking about while you are doing something. Only those particularly trained to perform this trick, or those with special talents in this direction, can be sources for the data' (1983: 289).

There are three interesting aspects to this criticism. The first is that a protocol gives unreliable data, because one protocol cannot show with what consistency a writer will use a characteristic mix of processes for different kinds of writing on different topics on different occasions for different audiences. This is a criticism of 'one-shot' data collection procedures, not of protocol analysis *per se*. The second is that talking while writing is a very specialized task, and therefore any composition process highlighted in it may only be characteristic of that task and not typical of the writer's normal way of operating when not talking about it at the same time. A possible check on this would be the resemblance of the written product to that writer's normal style, for if his or her normal writing processes were not being engaged it would be reasonable to suppose the written products would be different. The same objection was raised against protocol analysis of the reading skill, and validity checks have shown that, in reading, thinking aloud does not affect the process, but does extend the time needed. The third is that this specialized task can only be performed by certain individuals, who are either particularly talented or specially trained in self-observation, not the generality of writers, and that therefore the results of such research cannot be generalized to writers who do not have such special skills. It is certainly true that some respondents find little to say while writing and others can verbalize copiously. However, it does not seem that respondents have to be trained like performing animals, so to speak, to execute uncharacteristic feats. There is naturally individual difference here, but much useful information is available in the protocols. We have already encountered Smagorinsky's (1989) critical but positive account of the methodological problems in Chapter 1.

What L2 writers can tell us about their writing: case studies

There is now a small but solid published body of data from case studies of people writing in their second language. The two studies by Raimes (1985; 1987) and those by Lay (1982), Zamel (1983), Arndt (1987), Jones and Tetroe (1987), and McDonough (forthcoming) (see also the review by Krapels, 1990) contain information pertaining to unskilled writers in American college English programmes, relatively proficient Chinese learners of English in China, Venezuelan students in Canada trying to reach an acceptable TOEFL (Teaching of English as a Foreign Language) score for entry to a North American university, and English for Academic Purposes students in British universities. Students engaged on a wide range of writing tasks have been studied: narratives ('Tell me something unexpected that happened to you': Raimes, 1985); summaries of a set text; conventional topics such as writing about events or experiences or comparing an aspect of the two countries involved (Jones and Tetroe); writing suitable texts to fit specified endings (narratives and arguments: Jones and Tetroe); self-chosen topics. However, this range of tasks is still not wide enough to allow the measurement of the extent to which the character of the writing process changes according to the type of task set, which is a strong possibility. In terms of the product, Reid (1990) has already shown that compositions produced for the two different tasks used on the Test of Written English, a statement of comparison/contrast and a verbalization of graph material, differ considerably. Differences were found of overall length, pronominal reference, word length, and word category. No process measures were taken (it being a language-testing task – but see Chapter 5 for process studies of other language-testing modes). It would be interesting to know if different task specifications encourage different attentional foci during the writing process – on revising and altering the text, on the conception of the reader's possible interpretation, on planning or rehearsal, on text production. In terms of promoting unskilled writers to skilled writers, such effects could enable syllabus designers to ensure adequate development of all the sub-components of the writing process.

This body of data shows, as far as any generalization is possible in a field where individual differences are wide and marked, that second-language writers go through a number of fairly clear procedures: pre-writing, planning, rehearsing, etc. Pre-writing may take a short or a long time, but by and large it is a problem-solving activity whose aim is to sort out the meaning of the task set and some ways to approach it. Sometimes this means launching straight into a proposal for the text, sometimes it means sorting out a plan. There are some dramatic cases on record: Raimes's (1985) Yin Ping did not write anything for seventeen and a half minutes – all, however, devoted to exegesis of a single word in the set title. Raimes (1987: 451) describes a pre-writing sequence with which most of the studies agree: 'they read the question, often a few times, and with occasional rephrasing, then immediately rehearsed for writing. After a few associations, and after occasionally writing down a few notes, they said something about having to "begin with an introduction", and then began to write. They began writing without much prior consideration, even on complex issues.'

Planning moves occur sporadically throughout the time course of text generation. However, they are relatively few across all the studies. Raimes comments (and it is borne out in other studies) that planning tends to refer to 'learned prescriptions about essay form'. These are Flower and Hayes's 'Writing Plans in long term memory'. The use of such plans may help the students get back on course during the complex recursive process of writing; however, it may also affect adversely the solution of the problem, as in one of McDonough's summary writers, whose decision to treat each paragraph of the set text separately caused him to exceed the set maximum number of words twice over.

A feature of the comparison of the think-aloud protocols and the actual writing produced which is commented on by several authors is the frequent appearance in rehearsal of material which does not get incorporated in the final script, or, more unfortunately, a final script which is less comprehensible than it would have been if material actually rehearsed by the writer had indeed been included. Writers in an L2 apparently do not always discriminate between what they have set down on paper and what they have only thought or talked about.

There is indeed wide individual difference in the writing process. Johnson's unpublished study (1985) of six ESL students showed that her subjects approached the task in very different ways, depending on their proficiency in English, the language they normally encountered the topic in, and their personal educational histories.

Writing in two languages

A few studies have been able to look specifically at the comparison between writing in L1 and L2. Jones and Tetroe (1987), Lay (1982), and Arndt (1987) were able to do this. Jones and Tetroe, taking the quality of planning as an indication of writing skill, found that there was a high degree of consistency between the writers' behaviour in L1 (Spanish) and in the L2, English. Although there was also a correlation between the quality of planning and L2 proficiency, the low-proficiency subjects tended to do their planning in Spanish, in which language they had no linguistic inhibitions. Planning strategy, then, appeared to be a personal rather than a proficiency variable, and this result held good in general for their second writing task, composing a story to fit a given ending. Notable here, however, is that this task produces generally higher quantities of planning moves, though not necessarily at more abstract levels of planning. This is presumably because the cognitive problem of working backwards to provide a coherent piece of text is a greater puzzle than writing a free composition to a given title; but this cognitive problem is not well understood. It might have resulted from unfamiliarity with such a demand; completion tasks usually give a starting-point rather than a finishing-point. It may have been an inherent degree of complexity in the task of creating a coherent antecedent to a story-ending. Arndt also found a high level of consistency between the way her Chinese-speaking subjects approached the tasks in the two languages. The implication that these authors draw is that, at least in terms of kinds of plan people make and the kinds of overall strategy they adopt, cognitive processes which are characteristic of that person and which operate in their native language are transferred to the second language.

Friedlander (in Kroll, 1990*a*) investigated native speakers of Chinese, writing about a topic from Chinese culture, and one associated with the campus where they were working in the USA. He compared their planning and writing in the language associated with the topic (in Chinese for the Chinese topic and English for the US topic) and vice versa (in English for the Chinese topic and Chinese for the American one). These writers planned and wrote (they were assessed on both separately) better in Chinese about the Chinese topic than in English, and wrote better in English about the US topic than in Chinese; also, in general the quality of the essays on the Chinese topic were better in either language because of greater familiarity with the topic area. However, Friedlander's most interesting finding was the nature of the plans produced for the two different topic areas. For the Chinese topic, typical plans were short, lacking in elaboration, and relatively homogeneous; for the US topic, plans contained larger chunks of language, sometimes whole sentences, and much that later became incorporated as text, in whichever language they were directed to write. Furthermore, the plans were transformed into text in different ways. Short plans on a familiar topic became longer essays; long plans on the less familiar topic became shorter essays, regardless of the language of the plan or the product.

Friedlander's study is interesting and suggestive, but has to be treated with some caution, which he acknowledges. First, there may be an effect of culture or previous educational history which is idiosyncratic to these Chinese writers; second, the type of argument demanded in each topic was slightly different (comparison/contrast v. description); third, the task required both a plan and the text to be written in L1 or L2, and this may itself have conflicted with these writers' normal practice: other studies have noted that, during writing in the L2, little written planning occurs spontaneously in the pre-writing stage.

The work of Jones and Tetroe, Arndt, and Friedlander raises important questions about the role of both typical writing habits of planning and execution in L1 and of the use of L1 itself in planning and reflecting on the topic and the text. These are difficult decisions for a novice L2 writer to take: in Johnson's (1985) research, as in Friedlander's, the students used their L1 when planning text about traditions in their home countries and L2 more often when looking at current issues relating to their US campus life, but perceived using L1 as a hindrance for L2 writers of higher proficiency. Students may therefore perceive a difference in the usefulness or advisability of a novice strategy (using L1 for planning) for a more advanced stage of proficiency. On the other hand, Jones and Tetroe's subjects were more successful in writing in the L2 when at least some of their planning had been in L1, as the quality of those plans was higher.

Cultural factors

One might expect to find evidence of cultural barriers, or of the struggle to cross such divides in terms of culturally determined rhetorical patterns, in the think-aloud data produced by writers. This is a prominent, indeed controversial, feature of attempts to explain the rhetorical and some grammatical errors in non-native writing: that is, culturally bound rhetorical patterns are often inferred from analysis of written products. Connor and McCagg (1983) testify to this problem. Halimah (1991) showed that Arabic students learning to write for ESP maintained a rhetorical duality – a mixture of Arabic and English expository styles – by comparing their writing on the same topics in English and in Arabic. However, the students themselves hardly ever comment on this problem while doing their writing. This is true, for example, of both the Venezuelan subjects of Jones and Tetroe writing in the different cultural setting of Canada, my group of mixed origin writing in a British university, and the Chinese subjects of Arndt writing within their own cultural setting in Tianjin. It is of course consistent with the finding that planning strategies, particularly, are transferred between the two languages. This in itself could encourage transfer of culturally bound rhetorical patterns to writing in the second language, without this being the subject of conscious consideration. By and large, the data is silent on this matter, and this may be due to the natural self-selection of data in protocol analysis. Case-study work may be more forthcoming on this point: an ethnographic study by Galvan (1985) used in-depth interviews and observations to study the writing processes in English of graduate students born and schooled in Spanish in Latin America. Galvan claims that their (poor) performance in English reflected their uncertainty and oscillation between their L1, thought patterns, and culture and their L2 and the thought patterns and culture associated with it. A case-study by James (1984) of a single Ph.D. student from a Latin American country studying in the UK similarly reveals wide discrepancies between the writer's beliefs about the meaning of details of his text and his native speaker reader's, and between his conceptions of the nature and purpose of the academic argument he is presenting and the academic context in which he is presenting it.

Reviewing, revising, and editing

All writers read over what they have written: *reviewing*, in Flower and Hayes's terminology, takes up a great deal of time. However, it is done for a number of different purposes. In some cases it is simply to provide a springboard for the next segment of writing, the process proceeding as a series of 'two steps forward, one step back'. In a few cases, whole sections are reread before a new section is attempted. In yet other cases, the writers seemed to get a 'running start' (Raimes, 1985: 247) from the previous few words, and use that backtracking to get the opening phrase of a new sentence, only to stop again and rehearse what the new sentence was going to be about. In free composition, however, it is remarkable that reading over what has been written is only rarely associated with revising and editing; these activities tend to occur as part of the general uncertainty of committing sentences to paper. In other words, revising moves tend to be an integral part of the text production, not the outcome of reading over whole sections of text. Summarizing seems to encourage reviewing and editing moves: McDonough's summary writers read over sections of their texts more often, and made more text changes, in their summaries than in their free compositions.

Most studies of the L2 writing process acknowledge the seminal work of Faigley and Witte (1981) as the starting-point for the study of revising. They looked at L1 writers in the process of refining their texts and found, by using a text analysis, confirmation of what Sommers (1980) had found by using interview data. Inexperienced writers tend to revise less than experienced writers. However, neither the quantity nor the particular types of change made are necessarily the significant variables: it is the effect of the revisions that demarcates the difference between experienced and inexperienced writers. Thus the revisions made by inexperienced writers often do not improve their texts, and possibly do damage to the text. Faigley and Witte commented: 'Success in revision is intimately tied to a writer's planning and reviewing skills.' There are many instances in the L2 reports which support this contention. In the first place, most revision is at a local, surface level, of spelling, morphology, and word choice. Second, it does not necessarily improve the text for the reader (though one should assume the writer perceives it as an improvement). The inexperienced L2 writer evaluates his or her text according to criteria that are not yet those of a reader: the skill of putting themselves into their reader's shoes, of reading their own text as if shorn of the extra meaning which they believe and hope is there, and was perhaps rehearsed but ultimately left unexpressed, is a late one to develop. Flower (1979) has already noted this reluctance to move from 'writer-based' to 'reader-based' prose in L1 novice writers, noting the attractiveness and logic of writer-based prose for writers. She conceives of the task as a move from writing as an 'interior monologue' to a set of transformations – for example, to a consideration of the reader's purpose in reading, selecting a focus of mutual interest, using concepts rather than facts and details, and choosing an appropriate text structure.

Gaskill (1986) investigated revising strategies in Spanish and English as an L2 among university students of two proficiency levels in English. He conducted observations and think-aloud sessions. Consistent with other studies, his writers revised more in the process of producing drafts than between drafts; most of the alterations in either language were about surface details rather than organization or meaning. He drew an interesting conclusion for writing pedagogy: that the more proficient writers needed guidance on how to revise their texts with a hostile or unsympathetic reader in mind, whereas the less proficient needed guidance on how to generate and develop ideas to include in their writing. Another researcher, Rorschach (1986), noted that L2 writers' modes of conceiving of their readers are not well understood, and neither is how the writer makes planning and revising decisions in the light of his or her concepts of the reader. Rorschach's own research showed that, as L2 writers produced further drafts of their writing, their revisions concentrated more on surface details and less on alterations of organization and content designed to present ideas succinctly to a reader. Rorschach suggested, on the basis of outside readers' evaluations of her subjects' work, that these writers were attempting to conform increasingly strictly to an imposed essay structure, rather than revise their writing for the purpose of communicating to an audience. In terms of Flower and Hayes's model, the weak link in the process here is the use of previously used plans for writing rather than knowledge of the intended audience, thus highlighting a possible conflict between different kinds of representation stored in long-term memory.

An example of a think-aloud protocol: talking while writing

An example may help to focus the discussion so far. This writer was writing a composition on a general topic, the differences between studying English in his own country and in the UK. He was asked to think aloud into a language laboratory cassette recorder, after being given a demonstration and participating in a group discussion of writing under such conditions. He was a member of a group of volunteers participating in a study of free composition and summary writing in L2. This particular writer rehearsed aloud about what he might say under the given title for nearly fifteen minutes, in English, not his native language, before beginning to write anything. This rehearsal is more of a collection of themes than a plan of how the ideas will be presented in the finished product. We join this stream of consciousness at the point where the writer decides to set some of these ideas down on paper for the first time. In this example, words in italics indicate when the writer was speaking while writing or self-dictating, and these words became the final handed-in version after reviewing.

1 what . . . hm . . . how do I have to write something
2 speaking at the same time oh my god . . . so about that ok

3 a summary of that ah ... oh ... *the difference between*
4 *studying English in England and in my own country*
5 *are that firstly* firstly *in England I can* I can *I*
6 *can talk to native* native *speakers as much as I want*
7 *and* secondly no before that *this means* this means
8 *environment itself* environment itself is is *fit for*
9 *English study* English study *and secondly* secondly
10 secondly I can do we can *I have to* have to *adapt*
11 *myself living with* living with *English ... it is*
12 *essential for me using English regardless of making*
13 *mistakes* making mistakes regardless of making
14 mistakes ah regardless of making mistakes or making
15 making em mistakes or making shame making shame
16 ... *on the other hand* other hand *in Japan* em we or I
17 not we only *I used to study English just for*
18 *academic achievement* ment for *examinations. I*
19 *didn't have to ... study it so that I could be an*
20 *English speaker. The quantity of vocabulary are*
21 *limited or I didn't have to try to learn* learn to
22 try learn *by heart whatever words I came across and*
23 *even if I* even if I studied no I *had studied*
24 *English* it's no it *with great enthusiasm I would*
25 *not have had enough opportunity to use it in real*
26 *life.* and er I have to quote something from my real
27 life or my real experience here so *Although I* I
28 *studied English about 6–8 years in schools* in
29 schools *from 13 years* years *old* when I come here
30 *when I first come* when I first come England I *I*
31 *wasn't able to catch and recognize what people said*
32 *but the more I spent my time here in England the*
33 *more I could catch the sound* sounds *of English* of
34 English *and meaning* meanings *themselves* meanings
35 themselves *Indeed* indeed *to study any language* any
36 language *in native countries gives us rapid*
37 *progress of language ability but we shouldn't* we
38 shouldn't *forget advantages of studying* advantages
39 of studying of studying *language in our own*
40 *countries* our countries *because we can* we can
41 *build up the language ability* ability we can build
42 up the language ability *in stable environment* or
43 circumstances circumstances hm *although* although
44 although although it *it takes us quite a long time*
45 *and too much effort to to study completely the*
46 *language ...*

A number of features of this protocol illustrate the kinds of insights that can be achieved by this method of research, and also some of the drawbacks.

Text production occurs in a mixture of long sequences and single words interrupted by repetitions and comments. This is typical of most writers so studied: there is a fluent style (e.g. ll. 16–23) and an incremental style (e.g. ll. 33–5), and most people use both at different times. What allows some ideas to be produced fluently and others not is not clear. First, in many cases what has been rehearsed beforehand is easier to encode fluently; but on the other hand many ideas that are rehearsed never make it on to paper, even though there is no discussion actually rejecting them. Second, production is often interrupted by apparently trivial worries about surface forms.

This writer also demonstrates the phenomenon of the *running start*. At several points the actual writing finishes with an introductory word, after which more repetition or rehearsal occurs, presumably to find the appropriate way to encode the idea that the writer wanted to introduce but hadn't planned: e.g. 'and secondly' (l. 9); 'and even if' (ll. 22–3); 'indeed' (l. 35).

Revisions occur for this writer as part of text production; and although he did read the whole text through at the end, only one revision was made at that point. The most significant revision in this extract concerns 'making mistakes' (ll. 13–16). Here, a good phrase is repeated five times after writing it and eventually changed into a phrase with poor lexical cohesion ('making shame'), but with a much stronger revelation of the author's feelings about the point. This is the only point queried again in the final read-through, where it reverts in fact to 'making mistakes'. Several other alterations are made at surface level, e.g. 'we or I not we' (ll. 16–17); 'even if I studied no I had studied' (l. 23); 'it's not it' (l. 24); 'sounds', 'meanings' (ll. 33–5). This writer is clearly monitoring his own text production, and is in any case a relatively accurate writer from a technical morphological point of view. There are, naturally, several errors that do not get corrected and which are preserved in the final version.

This writer – rated as quite proficient – seems to have no problem with the organization of his text at the point of utterance. Almost all his written sentences are introduced by cohesive markers, and these are not inserted on reviewing the passage but occur as part of initial text production. Moreover, they are not altered in the light of the points that are written down subsequently. It is as if this writer uses cohesion markers as navigational indicators, often pausing at them to decide how to proceed to the next one, but not rethinking the course of his argument for the purposes of revision. This implies a writing plan somewhere, but it is not announced or written down. During his initial rehearsal, he talks at one point about a draft; but although this contains many of the points that appear in the writing, the structure within which those points are framed is not discussed. That structure runs schematically as follows:

Topic announcement: *differences*
Examples: *firstly* (talking to native speakers), *secondly* (adapt to living with the language)
Contrast: *on the other hand* (in Japan, learning for academic purposes)
Condition: *and even if* (impossibility of learning fluency)
Concession: *although* (school experience, couldn't understand English in UK)
Contrast: *but* (England residence made it easier)
Intensification: *Indeed* (rapid progress in L2 country)
Contrast: *but* (advantages of learning in stable L1 environment)

The only point at which this structure is modified while writing is the postponement of the second example (ll. 7–8, 'secondly no before that') to include the point about the environment (in England) being 'fit' for English study – a point that is actually absent from his final draft.

Most of this writer's verbalizations on think-aloud are text, repetitions of text, or edits of text. Occasionally there are also comments about the process itself. In this extract there are two: first, the decision to start writing, followed by the realization that he has to continue talking while doing it, which does not seem to give him much trouble once he starts; and second, the reminder to himself (ll. 26–7) to put in something about his own experience – a point that had not, in fact, been part of his original rehearsal of ways of composing an answer to the question. For this writer the think-aloud situation is itself worthy of comment, as for many respondents. His behaviour is consistent in that, having rehearsed rather than outlined at the beginning, he is not constrained only to write the points he originally thought of – but adding a new point from his own experience is nevertheless marked by a comment. In this way the protocol demonstrates both the recursive features noted by Perl, but the large amount of repetitions and the recycling of material rehearsed at the beginning, and also the 'orchestration' noted by Flower and Hayes, by the incorporation of new points constrained by what has gone before and the ideas still to be expressed.

What is absent is any comment about the reader of his prose – presumably because no addressee other than the 'default' addressee, the teacher (in this particular case the researcher), is imagined. In other research, it has been noted that even where instructions are given to address particular readers ('Imagine you are writing for the readers of X magazine'), it is the teacher who is written for. This writer makes no comments, but does include background information about learning in his own country and the nature and purpose of language learning there, which might not constitute shared presuppositions between him and his supposed reader.

Feedback

Closely allied to revision and editing strategies is the writing teacher's intervention by way of feedback. There have been several studies which have asked students in different ways how they use the feedback provided by teachers. In a study by Zamel (1985) displaying some elements of 'action research', the ambiguous nature of many comments on the content and form of students' written work is highlighted, and disturbing evidence was found of students' fair copies, i.e. papers rewritten after receiving feedback, being either no better or actually worse than the original as a result of the feedback. In her study, both the teachers' comments and the students' rewrites were collected as part of the normal process of teaching. No account was taken of the students' opinions about the feedback nor of the students' exercise of choice as to whether to incorporate it in a fair copy. In a study by Cohen (1987; 1991), a questionnaire was used in order to see how many students used the comments made by the teachers and in what ways. In fact some 17 per cent of his sample of New York State University students on various kinds of course did not read over their teachers' comments anyway. The majority did so, but the action they took varied between 'making a mental note' only, which was indeed the majority, to working out the corrections and rewriting. Cohen compared the actions reported by the students with their own evaluations of themselves as L2 writers. Over half of those who rated themselves as excellent writers simply used the strategy of 'making a mental note'. By contrast, the strategies of those students who thought of themselves as poor writers were more evenly distributed between that strategy, actual rewriting, and writing out some of the points commented on. However, the self-rated better writers paid more attention to vocabulary, grammar, and mechanics of writing than did the self-rated poorer writers. Thus, writers' self-evaluation of proficiency correlates with the kind of work they are prepared to do on their text following comments by their teacher.

Radecki and Swales (1988), also using a questionnaire but adding an interview with selected writers, coined the terms 'Receptors' and 'Resistors' to describe the individual characteristics of students who were willing to act on the feedback given and those who were not. The Receptors welcomed the ESL instructors' comments about organization, ideas, and content, and were willing to use the instructors' hints on how to revise their grammar. Several of them were able to review their own writing critically. By comparison, the Resistors and an intermediate group of Semi-resistors manifested a number of attitudes that hindered the teachers' attempts at helpful feedback: for example, they tended to associate re-writing 'with failure and punishment, equating it with surface-level correction', and refusing to review their own products in terms of rhetorical organization of the argument. Radecki and Swales warn that, however, in their research there is no identification of Receptors and Resistors with better or poorer writers; the relationship between receptivity to feedback and proficiency in writing is complicated by the aims of the student and the type of course they are following, for example a language course or a course in another academic subject for which English is needed as a 'service' language. The behaviour of the different groups may be a reflection of a more general individual difference of locus of control, between self-directed and other-directed people.

Cohen and Cavalcanti (1987; 1990) have also looked at student attitudes to feedback and the use made by students of the teachers' comments, in three different teaching contexts in Brazil. A striking result of this study was the relatively high percentage of comments which students either did not understand or did not know how to handle – mainly between a third and a half of all teacher comments, irrespective of whether the student was a low, intermediate, or high performer in writing. In one instance, a high performer received a total of two comments, neither of which he felt he could do anything about or with, nor probably wanted to. In this context, it is important to note that teacher comments on student text constitute a genre of their own, and may have a number of diverse purposes:

- to justify a mark
- to show the student how to improve the text
- to remind the student of past, familiar errors
- to give the student an indication of the effect of the text on a reader
- to suggest ways of tackling writing about a fresh topic.

Not all marginal comments are to be read in the same way; the effectiveness of the comment depends to some extent on the student understanding its intention, and this is only possible within a shared framework of expectations and task demands.

In a study oriented to the written product, Fathman and Whalley (1990) showed that comments focused on grammatical form are more successful in promoting changes than comments focused on content; but this study did not look at the central concern of this chapter, the writing processes of the student. For this reason there is no explanation for Fathman and Whalley's results in terms of writing processes or learning strategies. Their study used a balanced design, but was not embedded in a particular classroom context; and so the rewriting stage required was not necessarily a normal part of their various ESL classes, and the restricted feedback given in the experimental situations was necessarily different from the normal treatment of the essays by the teachers. The contrast between this product-oriented study and Cohen and Cavalcanti's process-oriented study was noted by Cohen; it serves to complicate an already fluid picture.

Summary and implications

This chapter has presented a number of current ideas about the processes involved in learning to produce written text in a foreign language. The protocol analysis method has enabled researchers to gradually put together a view of how L2 writers plan, rehearse, revise, and edit their texts, and in some cases process comments from their teachers, the usual *de facto* reader. It is clear that novice L2 writers have a great deal to tell us about how they go about the task and about what they do with their teachers' attempts to help them. Many themes have been broached: the quality of planning, the role of the L1, the quality and quantity of revision, writers' conceptions of the reader or audience, the relation between proficiency and ways of processing feedback, the nature of the genre of teacher comment, the nature of text production. None of them has yet received final or indeed adequate descriptions: there is a role for more research in all of these issues, and a case for extending the scope of the research to other kinds of language learner, for most of the work described here has concerned college-level writers in either L1 or L2.

An underlying theme of the chapter has been that we are unlikely to make progress in devising successful ways of teaching writing in a foreign language or to plan effective methods of training writing teachers unless we develop the means to hear what the students can say. The protocol analysis and think-aloud studies assembled and described in this chapter represent a foundation of work on this problem which needs expansion and refinement, targeted at many more writing situations and writing tasks.

It is also worth noting that the processes described in the writing studies are of a different quality from those already encountered in the discussions of reading and receptive skills and of planning and compensatory strategies in talking. Elements of the writing process have been isolated by reference to the L1 work of Flower and Hayes and Perl, and gross categories such as planning and revising have been investigated. In the reading literature, the delineation of strategies has been taken from inspection of what the readers said while they were reading; while there is considerable overlap and common ground between different pieces of research, there is also much greater scope for individual or even idiosyncratic strategies and mix of strategies to appear. In the speaking literature, there has been an emphasis on compensation for mutual linguistic inadequacy for the topic; the writing literature does not manifest such a concern to the same kind of degree. It may be that this reflects the different nature of the exercise of the skills involved. Writing, even if handed in for receiving comments, stands in a different time relation to its likely comprehension or incomprehension by the reader; the need for immediate compensation within the message is lacking. Similarly, the writer is in an important sense in control of the text in a way that a reader is not; approaches that somehow equate the two tasks, because they both involve communication in the written language, miss this dimension, and risk losing sight of the very important differences revealed by asking people what they are thinking about as they read or write text.

5

Learning to learn and teaching to learn

Introduction

The three preceding chapters have presented the fruits of research into learner strategies in the traditional four skill areas. This chapter will investigate learner and learning strategies in a more general sense, looking at the beliefs about the learning task that students report, the ways they organize themselves and evaluate their learning performance, the ways they differ, and the manner in which they respond to being taught learning strategies. The chapter will be presenting both descriptive studies and interventionist studies, looking at what learners tell us about the learning task and at what studies tell us about the success of attempts to get learners to adopt particular options.

In discussion of learner strategies, a number of levels are discernible. It is as well to introduce these at this point for clarity. We have already met the concept of learning strategy in the work of Tarone, who (see Chapter 2) distinguished it from communication strategy on the one hand and production strategy on the other. A learning strategy, called by some authors a 'cognitive' strategy, thus serves as a means for the student to increase his knowledge of the language by some manipulation of the language data presented (like repeating it or devising a mnemonic for it). One might imagine that beyond this there is also a level of strategy for organizing oneself as a learner – and we have already met Carrell's use of the term 'metacognitive strategies'. Later in this chapter we shall look closely at the suggestion that above these metacognitive strategies there is a level more akin to belief than to action – the preconceptions about language and learning that students bring to the task or which they develop as a result of their learning experiences. These three kinds of cognitive characteristic are internal to the learner – and indeed may never be expressed unless the student is actually asked about them – but may exert a powerful influence on the student's route and rate of learning. There is, however, a fourth set – the social strategies. We have already encountered an example – Tarone's

Table 5.1

Internal	External
Beliefs	Social-affective strategies
Metacognitive stategies	
Cognitive strategies	

'appeal for assistance' category of communication strategy. These kinds of cognitive characteristic can be set out as shown in Table 5.1.

Eight questions about learning strategies

The arguments in this chapter can best be summarized as a set of eight questions. In the main body of the chapter we shall see what empirical research can do to find answers to these questions, and in the final section we shall review the field to draw some conclusions about the questions. A number of the questions that follow have arisen already from the previous discussion of skill areas.

1. How do learners conceptualize the task?

Student beliefs about the task of learning a language feature quite strongly in a number of pieces of research. Two in particular have attempted to systematize, in different ways, these beliefs – those in Horwitz (1987) and Wenden (1987). These two studies, using a questionnaire and a protocol analysis method respectively, will be compared later. One of the major difficulties of research in this area, and one we have met before, is maintaining the distinction between analysis and intervention. It is in the nature of these beliefs that for many people they are difficult to formulate, so asking people about them is itself a kind of intervention. There is the ever-present danger that asking someone to give his view about an aspect of his own behaviour risks the creation, not merely the report, of the attitude.

2. When is a strategy good?

We have already seen that strategies are not necessarily good in themselves: almost any strategy can lead to failure if used inappropriately. In particular, the studies of Cohen and Aphek in the classroom and Sarig on reading have highlighted the 'hit-and-miss' nature of strategy use. The question is important, however, when one turns from description to intervention: if strategy use is being recommended or being taught to students, then it is vital to establish how and in what circumstances, and perhaps for whom, the strategies being recommended actually work.

3. Do process strategies become learning strategies?

The issue here is whether strategies for, say, interpreting the written word, or controlling the writing of a composition, can become strategies for learning more language. It is often thought to be the case, but it is not a necessary connection. A learner may normally use a glossary to make out a word in a reading text – but that does not of itself ensure that he or she will remember that word.

4. Do compensatory strategies produce learning?

We have seen that, in the area of communication strategies, the use of such strategies to compensate for a perceived lack of linguistic resources or for an actual or feared breakdown of communication is so important as to be criterial in the definition of strategy for some authors. However, it is less obvious what a student learns by using such a device. There is a general advantage in overcoming the possible breakdown of communication, and therefore keeping the channel of communication open. To a non-native speaker this is an achievement in itself and brings the benefits, in most cases, of maintaining the topic. The main benefit is actually conversing, in a simple sense of exchanging information, and thereby maintaining the attention of a conversation partner for further practice in real-time language use. It is doubtful, however, if using a compensatory strategy such as word coinage or approximation leads to retaining the correct linguistic form even if the interlocutor supplies it. Even in the case of appeals for assistance, there is no guarantee that the linguistic forms supplied will be remembered just because they were first encountered in this way.

In the case of receptive strategies for reading and listening, we have seen that top-down strategies may be compensatory for lack of automatic knowledge of word meaning. In this case, however, the use of context can be seen as an instance of computational effort to puzzle out the meaning of a word, and might therefore lead to the retention of the previously unknown word, on the argument that memory partly depends on the amount of work performed. On the other hand, contextual guessing often leads only to a satisfactory general interpretation of the sentence in which the unknown element occurs, rather than to an identification of a meaning for a specific element, which is why, among other things, it is a weak mechanism for Krashen's (1982: 20–7) famous 'i + 1': the accretion of knowledge from instances of incomprehension embedded in the comprehensible.

5. Do learners learn learning strategies?

In other words, where do strategies for learning come from? Learning strategies may simply be the product of encountering similar problems repeatedly – like a 'learning set', or they might arise from the adaptation of general approaches to problem-solving situations outside the language field to second-language learning. Also, there may be a significant first-language influence.

Some years ago, individual-difference research was dominated by the concept of aptitude, or the talent for learning languages. Perhaps – research is not yet available to decide this question – rather than looking for an elusive 'talent' that can only be defined in terms of scores on tests that agree with each other and disagree with others ('convergent and divergent validity') we should be looking for a profile of the 'skilled learner'. O'Malley and Chamot (1990: 162–3) present a brief analysis of Carroll and Sapon's (1959) four main components of foreign-language aptitude in strategy terms, but present no evidence to validate it. A skilled learner would be one for whom the attributes outlined in Chapter 1 for doing certain kinds of skilled performance would be applicable to the activity of learning a foreign language. Bartlett (1958) years ago adapted the concept of psychomotor skill to thinking, and Anderson (1983) has expanded it to include a number of cognitive skills. O'Malley and Chamot (1990) present a detailed résumé of Anderson's theory with some applications to the field of second-language learning, locating the notion of learning strategies within the different kinds of knowledge and stages of learning proposed by Anderson.

6. Does teaching learning strategies produce better learners?

There is considerable interest in the idea of training learners to learn. We have already encountered it in terms of suggestions that teachers can use the identification of the strategies that good learners use, to select successful strategies to teach poor learners to use. It is sometimes called 'learner training', and sometimes goes under the banner of 'language awareness'. There are good reasons, supported by promising empirical evidence, to think it should be successful. However, as we have already seen in part, there are a number of problems with this argument. First, it is not clear that what differentiates good and poor learners is the choice of strategy; it may simply be the range and amount of use of strategies. Second, there are constraints on when a strategy works which are to do with individuals, possibly cultural background, type of problem, and proficiency level. Third, a pedagogic decision of some risk has to be taken to devote teaching time to strategy training rather than language learning, and the pay-off is not secure.

7. How wide is individual variation?

There are important individual differences in all of these matters; in describing general trends and major successes and failure one should not overlook idiosyncracies and the breadth of individual experience.

8 What about the teacher?

Teachers are involved in learning strategies in two obvious ways: knowing about, supporting, managing, and occasionally teaching, the strategies used by their students; and using a range of strategies of their own. On the first, there is a strategy instruction proposal referred to as the Strategic Teaching Model (Jones *et al.*, 1987; quoted in O'Malley and Chamot, 1990) for subject teaching in the first language: O'Malley and Chamot discuss this and several other models, including their own CALLA (Cognitive Academic Language Learning Approach), in terms of adapting the proposals for developing course work in second-language learning strategies. On the second, there is relatively little work on the interactive side of learning strategies in instructed language learning, but it is an important aspect; there is very little research on the strategic behaviour of teachers, although it is obvious that there is wide individual difference in the procedures that individuals adopt to accomplish the same classroom ends.

Descriptive studies

The earliest large-scale study to look at learning strategies in a foreign or second language was that of Naiman *et al.* (1978, but performed in 1974–5), referred to as the 'Good Language Learner' (GLL) study. The aim of this study was to investigate the foreign-language learning processes of secondary- (high-) school pupils learning French in nominally English-speaking Canada. Part of the aim was to validate Stern's (see Chapter 1) list of strategies for foreign-language learning by enquiring to what extent learner's success was associated with them. The study was interesting partly, also, for its multi-method research design, because it used individual difference questionnaires and other tests – notably the Embedded Figures Test for Field-Independence or Dependence, interviews with adults and school learners, class observation, and language proficiency measures.

The correlational part of the study – identifying how measures of individual differences derived from general psychology ranged as a function of their proficiency measures in French language – gave rise to a good deal of further work, discussed in McDonough (1981; 1986), and Skehan (1989), and elsewhere. For the present book, the interest in this important study lies in the attempt to validate the general learning strategies proposed by Stern (1975) and derived in part from Rubin (1975), and referred to earlier as 'wholesome attitudes' rather than problem-solving strategies. In order to do this, these researchers collapsed the original list of ten to six which could be more reliably distinguished from each other; they looked for evidence for them in the interviews which they held with learners, and also in the observations of the learners in the classes. As others have found, the attempt to observe strategies in action was not successful – indeed, the class observation did not show up much in common with the other individual difference measures either, a persistent difficulty with that kind of research. However, the kinds of thing the interviewees disclosed about themselves did give a lot of information bearing on the use of these strategies. In reading the following examples, taken from Naiman *et al.* (1978: 50, table 6), one should bear in mind that this was not 'think-aloud' research in the sense discussed in earlier chapters; what the interviewees said was stimulated by an interviewer's questions and required retrospection, with all of the attendant uncertainties and difficulties.

Strategy 1: The GLL finds a style of learning appropriate to him by initially conforming to the learning situation or effectively adapting it to his personal needs. In the process of his language learning he learns to identify personal preferences regarding the way he should like to learn a language and selects learning situations accordingly.

(Subject #12 accepted the rigid way of learning at High School, as this method provided him with the foundations for different languages; the method demanded rote learning, memorizing and learning by heart on the student's part.)

(Subject #23 knows – through her previous language learning experience – that she needs structure and organization, especially at the beginning, and both formal and informal settings to learn a foreign language. Before immersing herself in the target language, she would, for example, take a crash course; in addition to the informal learning situation in the country itself, she would continue with formal instruction.)

Strategy 6: The GLL realizes initially or with time that he must cope with the affective demands made upon him by language learning.

(Subject #4 overcame inhibition to speak 'just by doing it', by getting herself into situations where she had to use L2.)

(Subject #15: when learning a language 'You've got to be able to laugh at your own mistakes, you've got to have a sense of humour'.)

(Subject #28: 'You simply have to sit down and work out a way that you can do it and spend a lot of time at it and expect not to get very far for a while and expect to have lots of setbacks and get boring work a lot of times.')

Naiman *et al.*'s collection of case-studies of learners in schools, where the authors both interviewed and observed over quite extended periods (five hours of class instruction or so) makes fascinating reading, but the material is too long to reproduce here, and cannot sensibly be summarized or reduced to tabular form. The general context of this research was exploratory; it is conspicuous that the student case-studies, which are mainly cases of mismatch between performance and ability, cannot draw on any results in the main body of the research for explanation.

There have been many criticisms directed against this work: the proficiency measures have been considered suspect (the International Educational Assessment (IEA) listening test and an oral repetition task); the study searched for evidence to validate a list of strategies distilled from general psychology, rather than classifying and interpreting the strategies talked about spontaneously by the respondents; the personality trait measures were not followed up in the design of the classroom observations; the strategy evidence was not taken from students actively engaged in language using or learning tasks but from retrospections and reflections; and so forth. But the Canadian study was enormously important in its time, and opened up many research questions which several studies conducted in the 1980s continued to pursue.

For example, an introspective case study of two successful learners was conducted by Gillette (1987). Gillette observed two independent-minded successful learners of French and Spanish as foreign languages in class, interviewed them, and obtained questionnaire data from them about their motivation. No very sophisticated techniques were used in data collection or analysis: the researcher asked the students what they thought. She categorized the data resulting from these three sources under five headings: motivation, personality, socio-cultural variables, cognitive variables, and learner strategies. Both of these students turned out to be motivated integratively (in the weak sense of 'generalized interest in foreign languages'); tolerant of ambiguity; risk-takers; with high self-esteem; all traits commonly associated with success (although not necessarily a cause of it); and possessed of above-average social inquisitiveness, although one was very low on ethnocentrism and the other apparently believed in American geopolitical superiority. However, the last two categories, cognitive variables and learner strategies, are the most interesting from the present point of view. They both reacted seriously to class instruction, with active involvement, silent and aloud, using mental rehearsal as well as active responding. They were both highly aware of their own learning strategies and behaviour, possibly associated with their high levels of self-esteem evident from their questionnaire responses. Gillette describes their attitude as 'self-regulation'. Their learning strategies were independent and self-willed. Neither of them worried particularly about grades or imposed tasks, but concentrated on what they liked to do: attentive listening, trial and error; their attitudes to error were relaxed and almost welcoming (M: 'If I don't understand everything, I will try to make a hypothesis with what I've got') with one of them, R, using errors as an aid to acquisition.

After describing her two subjects as successful learners, Gillette is, however, cautious not to recommend others to be taught to follow in their path (1987: 278):

Most importantly, R. and M. are in full control of their own learning process. Rather than being dominated by their school environment, R. and M. adapt it to their individual purposes and never look for language learning 'recipes' developed by others. Consequently, it does not seem appropriate to pass on a list of 'strategies' to be imitated. Instead, this study might encourage students to look more closely at their own behaviour in the foreign language classroom. Such an awareness is an important step towards becoming a successful learner.

Large-scale studies of L2 learning strategies

Another large-scale project was initiated and conducted by O'Malley and his associates in the mid-1980s, largely with English as a Foreign Language students and also with students of other foreign languages. Their work had three main components:

1. a development of cognitive learning theory, to encompass second-language learning, in order to provide the theoretical content which they considered was missing in, for example, the Canadian Good Language Learner work reviewed in the earlier section
2. descriptive studies of learning strategies used by ESL and other language students, and
3. interventionist studies of the success of teaching programmes designed to improve student language performance by teaching strategy use.

Here we will concentrate on the descriptive studies, commenting on the theoretical proposals in a later chapter and discussing the interventionist studies in the second main section of this chapter and from another perspective in the chapter on the classroom.

O'Malley *et al.* published a study (1985*b*) of learning strategy use by beginning and intermediate ESL students, which is also reported as Study 1 in O'Malley and Chamot's book (1990), and also written up in a rather briefer form by Chamot (1987) as her contribution to Wenden and Rubin's seminal collection of papers on 'Learner Strategies in Language Learning'. Some features of these authors' method of getting the data are noteworthy.

First, the study investigated both student strategies and teachers' ideas about their students' strategies, and also attempted to identify strategy use in classroom observations. O'Malley and his co-workers claim that theirs was the first study to ask teachers about their students' strategies, but in fact Naiman *et al.* had attempted this in a generalized fashion in the GLL study. Naiman *et al.* had found that teachers had had very little idea of what their students did (a finding echoed by Hosenfeld in a different context), and that the teachers tended to have rather stereotyped views of what good and poor learners did. However, it is possible that the interview method used in the Canadian study predisposed the respondents to answer from such stereotypes, as they were not being asked to think aloud during the process of teaching or conversing with the students. In the O'Malley *et al.* (1985*b*) study the yield, in terms of strategies identified from the student interviews, teacher interviews, and observations, was dramatically different, with the second two sources of data being so unproductive as to be negligible; the authors ignored them, and only reported the results of the student interviews in detail. In the case of the teacher interviews, there seems to have been a serious problem of confusion between student learning strategy and teaching strategy; in the case of the observations, there was simply not sufficient data. Unfortunately, the authors do not present any examples, in any of the reports of this study, of what the teachers said, nor any transcripts of the classes observed, so there is no opportunity for readers to satisfy themselves on this point. It is not a little surprising that the teacher interviews yielded so little, even if what they did yield could not be described as valid evidence of their students' strategies. Transcripts of the class observation might have revealed whether the lack of recognizable strategy use was due to the nature and methodology of the lessons (one might expect a drilling lesson to be relatively error-free and not give rise to obvious strategy use, whereas a group or pair discussion, using information and opinion gap exercises, might have provoked more), or to some characteristics of the group dynamics of the students (a particularly passive or strongly reflective group might yield less participatory strategies than a competitive or highly reactive group).

Second, the authors used a relatively large number of respondents – seventy students enrolled in ESL classes in high (secondary) schools, five of whom were Vietnamese speakers and the rest Spanish speakers. The researchers used the schools' definitions of proficiency, in which a beginner had 'little or no proficiency in English', and an intermediate had 'limited proficiency in understanding and speaking English and little or no skill in reading and writing English'. Both groups were deemed to need English in order to have a chance in the education system, otherwise they would not have been in the ESL classes. The beginners were withdrawn from mainstream classes to concentrate on English for the whole school year; the intermediates received two hours of English a day and a balance of mainstream courses. These details are quite important because each piece of research in this field yields, as we have seen, rather different results, and one reason for that is simply that each report is based on different kinds of student populations in different learning situations and stages of education. It is also evident that studies with fairly large numbers of respondents allow certain kinds of treatments – like numerical analysis and even simple statistical manipulations – which studies on a small group and on individuals do not.

Third, the students were not interviewed singly, but in groups of four or five, the beginners in Spanish, and intermediates in English.

Using a preliminary list culled from the previous literature, and inspection of the student interview data, O'Malley drew up a final list of strategies in three categories: *meta-cognitive*, *cognitive*, and *social-affective*. The full definitions of the list are given in Chamot (1987: 77), Rubin's book; on p. 33 of the original article by all the group; and O'Malley and Chamot (1990: 119–20), so there is no need to reproduce it in full here. In addition, Chamot (1987: 76–7) quotes some comments made by the students in interview, translated from Spanish (so presumably they were beginners), which illustrate the strategy categories:

METACOGNITIVE

Self-management: 'I sit in front of the class so I can see the teacher's face clearly.' 'It's a good idea to mix with non-Hispanics, because you're forced to practice your English. If you talk with a Chinese who is also studying English you have to practice the language because it's the only way to communicate.'

*Advance organization**: 'You review before you go into class. You at least look through each lesson. I don't try to totally understand it; I look over it.'

Self-monitoring: '. . . I just start talking. What happens is that sometimes I cut short a word because I realize I've said it wrong. Then I say it again, but correctly.'

Delayed production: 'I can more or less understand whatever is said to me now, but the problem is in talking. I need to study more so that I can talk better. I talk when I have to, but I keep it short and hope I'll be understood.'

COGNITIVE STRATEGIES

Imagery: 'Pretend you are doing something indicated in the sentences you make up about the new word. Actually do it in your head.'

Auditory representation: 'When you are trying to learn how to say something, speak it in your mind first. Then say it aloud. If it is correct, you can keep it in your mind forever.'

Transfer: 'For instance, in a geography class, if they're talking about something I have already learned [in Spanish], all I have to do is remember the information and then try to put it into English.'

---

* As such, this label does not occur in the list of definitions. The category, 'advance organizers', used only once in the whole sample, refers to a general but comprehensive preview; 'advance preparation', the most popular metacognitive strategy, refers to rehearsing linguistic items needed for a task.

Inferencing: 'Sometimes all the words of the sentences make the meaning of the new word. I think of the whole meaning of the sentence, and then I can get the meaning of the new word.'

They analysed their results in three different ways, which go some way to answering some of the questions posed at the beginning of this chapter, at least for this group of students.

Single strategies or multiple ones?

Most interestingly – and consonant with, for example, Sarig's work with students of much higher language-level reading in English as an L2 – a fifth of all the strategy uses reported by the students had to be categorized as 'multiple use'. In other words, these fairly low-level students were using combinations of strategies for a significant proportion of the time. Two-thirds of these instances were combinations of two cognitive strategies, a quarter were combinations of metacognitive strategies, and 7 per cent were combinations of metacognitive and cognitive strategies. The majority of the time, of course, was consumed by single-strategy use.

Strategy use and proficiency

The beginners reported rather greater use of strategies than the inter-mediates. It is very likely that this reflects the fact that the beginners were interviewed in their own language, and were therefore that much more forthcoming.

Both groups reported overwhelmingly more cognitive than meta-cognitive strategies; twice as many in the case of the intermediates and three times as many for the beginners. However, the metacognitive strategy use was substantial, and here the intermediates used more (34 per cent) than the beginners (27 per cent). Unfortunately, the researchers do not indicate the probability of obtaining this difference in proportions simply by chance, given this size of sample; oddly, in such a large-scale study, the numerical analyses remained crude, and no statistical tests were performed. We therefore have to regard this difference between the groups as unreliable. It would, of course, be interesting to claim that one thing that changes as one's proficiency in a language increases is one's use of meta-cognitive strategies – planning, monitoring, evaluating – but this study did not establish that as a fact.

By far the majority of the metacognitive strategies concerned planning the learning activities, particularly self-management, advance preparation, and selective attention. This was comparable in both groups. Student use of cognitive strategies also did not differ between the two groups. In order of frequency, they fell roughly into four groups (percentages in brackets):

Repetition, note-taking	(± 14)
Cooperation,* clarification questions	(± 12)
Imagery, translation, transfer, inferencing	(± 7)
Elaboration, key word, deduction, grouping, recombination	$(\geqslant 4)$

This order of frequency of use appears to mean that there is a cline of popularity from the rather mechanical kind of activity, through the engagement of somebody else's help, down to strategies involving a more active transformation of the material in a manipulative way. Students therefore used many strategies for coping with the language material, but the kind of work they were doing was not of a particularly efficient or sophisticated nature.

Strategy use and different learning activities

These students reported that they used strategies of various kinds for vocabulary learning most, then slightly less for pronunciation, less again for listening comprehension, social communication, and following instructions. This is consonant with the popularity of the simple, non-manipulative strategies of repetition and note-taking. O'Malley comments that one reason for the prevalence of vocabulary, pronunciation, and oral drills in provoking strategy use could have been the preponderance of these kinds of activities in the teaching they were receiving. One might add that (as was clear in the case of writing) task requirements are very influential in choice of strategy: O'Malley's methods of investigation appear to have precluded study of this variable. (The classroom observations are not reported.) It has to remain open if these students would, for example, have used a sophisticated elaborative strategy on the new vocabulary if the teaching method had required a more analytical approach, or whether they could not have responded in kind, at these low stages of proficiency.

Compared to the kind of strategy described in the earlier chapters on talking, reading, listening, and writing, these learning strategies are notable for one quality: they are decontextualized. O'Malley and Chamot's method of data collection attempted to avoid this by asking questions in the student interviews according to a strict sequence organized in terms of the nine learning activities selected. But the interviews took place after normal school hours, not in any juxtaposition to actual language-learning sessions, and the nine learning activities chosen for questioning do not seem to have borne any systematic relationship to the kinds of language-learning task employed by the teachers.

---

*The social strategy of cooperation was counted as a cognitive strategy for some reason – it is interesting that it shares the second most frequent group with questions for clarification.

Student perceptions of the learning task

Decontextualization raises problems if an attempt is being made to identify strategies for solving learning problems; but it may be a positive quality if researchers want their respondents to reflect on wider issues and reveal the beliefs that guide their choice of approach to learning. This is precisely what Wenden (1987) attempted to do. She interviewed a number of adult learners of English to find out 'what learners think about how best to approach the task of learning a second language – their explicit prescriptive beliefs'.

Rather than comb the transcripts of the interviews for instances of pre-defined strategies, Wenden used a rather different technique which she describes as 'content analysis'. This involved identifying themes in the transcripts which satisfied six criteria:

1. generalizations
2. justifications
3. either spontaneous or specific responses
4. signalling by verbal contexts
5. recurrence
6. detailed explanation

Using these criteria, Wenden isolated twelve themes and grouped them into three broad categories of students' prescriptions:

Group 1. Use the language
1. Learn the natural way
2. Practise
3. Think in your second language
4. Live and study in an environment where the target language is spoken
5. Don't worry about mistakes

Group 2. Learn about the language
6. Learn grammar and vocabulary
7. Take a formal course
8. Learn from mistakes
9. Be naturally active

Group 3. Personal factors are important
10. The emotional aspect is important
11. Self concept can inhibit learning
12. Aptitude is important

Wenden's work on language students' beliefs about the upcoming task is essentially a distillation of their own reported statements, and as such has a considerable degree of authenticity as prescriptive advice to other learners on 'How to be a successful language learner'. Wenden can justifiably argue that asking learners their own opinions is an advance on giving advice on the basis of one learner's or one teacher's experience. As usual, however, there are some problems with Wenden's approach in this study.

(a) She does not report any reliability check: thus, there is no comparison of her own interpretations of these transcripts of interviews with another independent reader or two (as performed by O'Malley and his coworkers, for example), nor does she report obtaining any kind of agreement from the sources of the data that her analysis fairly represents what they thought.

(b) Twelve statements extracted from this rich data seem rather small in number compared to Horwitz's (1987) thirty-four-item questionnaire (the Beliefs about Language Learning Inventory), which was based on teachers' opinions in a free-recall task and on small group discussions with students. According to Wenden, fifteen of Horwitz's questions coincide with her twelve themes; the rest are about other kinds of belief (e.g. about culture) which are excluded from her more restricted set.

(c) Overall, the themes that these adult learners highlight do not seem particularly surprising or novel. Wenden claims that they amount to the content of the students' 'theories in action' about language learning. Not all of the students agreed with all of the themes, so there is considerable individual variation, illustrated by Wenden with three case-studies. However, while these 'theories in action' may well guide these learners in their individual learning careers, they do not carry a great deal of explanatory power. There is no independent evidence of how consistent these learners' learning styles and learning activities are with their explicit beliefs.

Learner strategies reported and compared with action

Whereas Wenden's method of data analysis enabled her to compare interview transcripts and could be extended to other 'soft' evidence like personal learning diaries, it cannot answer the question posed above because it cannot look at the process of learning directly. A study of two individuals by Abrahams and Vann in the same collection (1987) attempted to do this. These researchers interviewed fifteen learners using a structured interview (a list of questions) and then asked them to perform four tasks which were supposed to be typical of their normal classroom activities, while doing a 'think-aloud' report. The tasks were a verb tense exercise, an article usage exercise, a Cloze test, and a writing composition. At the time of data collection, the researchers did not know which students would be successful in their language programme and which not. Abrahams and Vann report a detailed comparison of two of their subjects, one successful and one unsuccessful, who shared the same cultural and educational background and first language, Spanish. The interview with the successful G took two hours and twelve minutes, in which he mentioned 317 uses of 32 different strategies; that with the unsuccessful P took one hour and eleven minutes, in which he mentioned 81 uses of 19 strategies. It seems from the figures that strategy use by these high- and low-proficiency learners differed in both quantity and kind. In performing the tasks while thinking aloud, they revealed a number of differences which fitted the general picture, drawn by the authors, of the successful learner, G using many more communicative strategies than P, and in particular using more monitoring strategies. The unsuccessful learner seemed to take on the tasks in an impulsive and speedy fashion, not stopping to confirm the results of his puzzle-solving and being content with a superficial response.

It is important to note here that this research did not establish any direct relationship between what the subjects reported in the interviews and what they reported in the think-aloud task performance study: the authors noted that strategies revealed in task performance are usually highly specific to the task (as can be seen in the earlier chapters on broad skill areas). It is also important to remember that the correlation between strategy use and success which appears to be true of these two subjects is probably itself the result of obvious differences between them, and not evidence for a causal relationship. G was 33, a college lecturer with a degree; P was 20 and had graduated from high school only. It is furthermore noteworthy that, while they had been labelled successful and unsuccessful within the language programme they were enrolled in, their final scores on the TOEFL test were not as dramatically different as one might have expected: 523 and 473 respectively. Neither would have been recommended for entry to a British or North American university on that basis without further language instruction.

A scheme for strategies

Oxford (1990) describes a rather all-embracing scheme for learning strategy use, based on virtually all the previous work and used in developing the Strategy Inventory for Language Learning (SILL). Oxford's work uses a very wide definition of strategy, including almost any decision taken in the process of language learning. O'Malley and Chamot (1990) criticize this work as well they might, for its attempt at comprehensiveness and for the consequent removal of the various strategies so grouped from their original theoretical and empirical justifications. Oxford and her co-workers used this wide-ranging inventory in a large-scale factor analytic study with military personnel, discovering a consistent difference in the use of strategies by males and females. This issue had not been explored before because none of the previous pieces of research used sufficiently large numbers of subjects to be able to compare any sex-related variability with general variability. However, general caveats voiced earlier in the present text about the reliability of questionnaire data apply to this as to other large-scale studies.

Oxford *et al.* (1990) present six case studies of classrooms in which various kinds of strategy-teaching took place. Many of these are informal and not integrated in the normal teaching; common criteria for evaluating the outcomes are not applied; unfortunately, therefore, the value of these reports is limited.

Validity of strategy applications

An important study by Politzer and McGroarty (1985) related a number of interesting questions about the relationship between self-reported learning-strategy use and actual performance measures. Politzer and McGroarty carefully constructed a questionnaire instrument consisting of 'good behaviours' in language learning reflecting previous research in the 'Good Language Learner' tradition. It was divided into sections on classroom behaviour, individual study behaviours, and interaction behaviours. They administered it to a largish group (thirty-seven) of students enrolled in a pre-sessional English programme in advance of graduate study in the United States. The students came from two rather different kinds of culture (Asians and Hispanics), and they were intending to study engineering and social science or humanities, the majority of the Asians going for engineering and the majority of the Hispanics going for Humanities. They also tested the students on a number of measures at the beginning and end of the course, using a multiple-choice aural comprehension test (Plaister Aural Comprehension), a multiple-choice test of grammar (Comprehensive English Language Test for Speakers of ESOL), and a test of communicative competence based on productive responses to pictures of various kinds. In their results, it was clear that the Hispanics reported significantly greater use of 'good' learning strategies in all three sections of the questionnaire than the Asians. In many ways this is not surprising, since many of the supposedly good strategies are not valued as highly in Asian contexts as in the West, such as correcting fellow-students, volunteering, asking for help, asking the teacher questions. Politzer and McGroarty make the very important point that many of the 'good' learner strategies reported in the literature, particularly the social and interactional ones, reflect highly ethnocentric assumptions.

A second feature of their results was that the gains made by the Asians on the grammar test and the communicative competence test were significantly greater than those achieved by the Hispanics. On the aural comprehension test, the two groups gained about the same on average. Taken together, these two results are very disquieting for proponents of the view that there are learning strategies that are in some way inherently good for language-learning success: the group with the worse tally of good learning strategies performed better on the learning product measures. Here, the explanation most probably lies in the cultural and educational histories of the participating learners. It is also possible that the difference in intended subject of study, which coincided largely with cultural origin, might explain the result.

Politzer and McGroarty also found that there was no overall relationship between the group of learning behaviours in their questionnaire and the gains of the product measures. Rather, the only statistically significant differences occurred with ten individual questions. They concluded that this told them something useful about the different kinds of linguistic competence measured by the tests, but not very much about the learning behaviours themselves. Learning behaviours characterized by active enquiry, asking the teacher about an expression and asking for confirmation, correlated with gains in aural comprehension and communicative competence, but not with grammar; and behaviours indicating assiduity and keeping track of vocabulary, using new words in conversation, spending extra time practising words missed in class, were associated positively with gains on the grammar test but negatively with aural comprehension and communicative competence. They concluded that the view of learning strategies as being inherently good or bad for learning had to be abandoned: such strategies are normally much more restricted in effectiveness. This conclusion is neatly congruent with that of Cohen and Aphek, albeit drawn from a quite different kind of evidence.

The authors commented (Politzer and McGroarty, 1985: 118):

> Good language learning behaviour may, in the long run, be almost as elusive as good teaching behaviour. Depending on the level of proficiency or the frequency with which a particular behaviour is employed, the same learning strategy may be variously an intrinsically good learning behaviour, a sign of lack of progress, an indication of assiduity, and so on.

Interventionist studies

We now turn to the available evidence concerning teaching language students to adopt certain kinds of strategy or approach to learning, so that they might improve their language-learning performance. The descriptive studies, particularly the last one reviewed, have raised profound concerns about whether we know enough about learning strategies to warrant their incorporation in explicit teaching programmes. However, some studies of individual strategy use such as Hosenfeld's on reading have taken an explicitly interventionist approach, reporting considerable success, and in other academic areas strategy training has been practised for some time.

It is convenient to divide the studies on intervening by teaching strategies into a general group and a specific group. In the general group we shall look at studies which have aimed at teaching strategies for overcoming a number of learning problems encountered in several aspects of language learning; in the specific group we shall review what has been learned from attempting to teach particular strategies for, say, reading comprehension or vocabulary learning. In both groups the central questions remain the same:

- Can strategies be taught?
- Do students use the taught strategies?
- Do students who use the taught strategies perform better (than previously or than other students not so taught)?

Teaching strategies involves a number of decisions. Not all the research on strategy training has taken the same approach. In general, seven kinds of decision have to be considered:

1. Discover the student's strategies first or present the new strategies first.
2. Teach strategies and language together or separately.
3. Be explicit about the purpose of strategies or not.
4. Develop a course of training or a one-off lesson.
5. Choose the appropriate teaching techniques.
6. Choose a method of evaluation:
    improvement on learning task
    maintenance of strategy use after training
    transfer of strategy to new situations.
7. For an investigation of the strategy teaching, design an appropriate form of study:
    random assignment of students to tasks
    control group and control activities
    product measures and affective measures, etc.

General training

Wenden (1986; 1987) reports a study involving students on an intensive seven-week American language course, on which two of the twenty hours per week were devoted to discussion of language learning. These discussion hours were in fact planned as strategy training, through comprehension exercises and discussions based on texts for reading and listening passages, with homework consisting of practice tasks and focused diary writing. While some of the class time was being used for the strategy training and awareness-raising activities in this way, Wenden comments that the activities were not integrated as fully with the language training as, for example, the interventionist programme set up by Hosenfeld for reading.

Wenden's method of evaluation was by questionnaire, and by noting attrition rates: in fact a majority of the students did not want to continue the strategy training, and the questionnaire responses indicated that they saw it as irrelevant. She describes the participants as 'resistant'. One group that did persist did so mainly for the extra language practice it afforded. Subsequent modification of the course to integrate it more fully into the language training was apparently more successful in retaining the students' interest, but there was no attempt to evaluate its effectiveness either in raising the students' awareness of the issues or in improving their handling of the language material.

Following this rather disappointing study, O'Malley and his associates (1985a; 1987; 1990) performed two important studies, one with learners of English and one with learners of other modern languages. These studies were more complicated and better controlled. The intention was to discover what effect limited training about strategy use might have on students learning in a relatively normal classroom environment. In the first study, they used 75 students enrolled in suburban high schools, mainly from Spanish-speaking and Asian countries, with about a third from other language backgrounds. They divided the group into three subgroups, preserving the mixture of language, background and age (a 'nested random sample'). One subgroup received training in metacognitive, cognitive, and social-affective strategies; one in cognitive and social-affective; and one acted as a control group, directed to do whatever they normally would with the material. Students were taught in groups of eight to ten. This procedure, while necessary for the experimental method, effectively destroyed the students' normal class membership, so the relevance of the results for 'normal classes' can be questioned. The strategy training continued for a class hour per day for eight days. The training was integrated with instruction in three language tasks.

O'Malley et al. (1985a; 1987; 1990) compared the improvement on the language tasks in three groups, and related these to the strategy training. On the speaking task, the group given training in all three kinds of strategy improved significantly more than the control group, with the group given training only on cognitive and social-affective strategies somewhere in between the two. To obtain such a result in such a short trial (eight days of training, presumably ten or eleven calendar days only, separating the pre-test from the post-test) is remarkable. It is possible that the gains achieved might have reflected the unfamiliarity of the task on pre-test, and not the students' general oral proficiency, but this could not explain the differences in improvement in the three groups.

On the listening task, no overall improvement could be attested, perhaps because the tasks were too difficult, or perhaps because the reminders to use the taught strategies for listening were omitted early in the training. There were some improvements in particular tasks.

On the vocabulary task (curiously, not reported in 1985*a*) no overall improvements by group were found – but there was, so to speak, a cultural difference. The Asian students in the control group used rote repetition, and the Asian students in the strategy training groups resisted the training, preferring to use what was natural to them: the control group was more successful. By contrast, the Hispanic students in the strategy training groups improved more than the Hispanic students in the control group, apparently preferring to learn alternative strategies. This result strongly underlines the warning sounded by Politzer and McGroarty concerning the cultural bounds of learning strategies and the risks of interfering with them.

The second study, by Chamot, Küpper, and Impink-Hernandez (1988, quoted and described in detail by O'Malley and Chamot, 1990: 175–84), attempted to evaluate the effects of persuading regular teachers of Russian and Spanish to add into their regular classes a component of learning strategy instruction. The method of evaluation used in this study was not improvement in the students' actual language proficiency, as in the previous study, but observation by the researchers of particular language classes. The researchers discussed the typical learning strategies of the students with the teachers beforehand. Learning strategies to be focused on in the classes on listening and reading comprehension and oral skills were selected, and the teachers devised lessons integrating this learning strategy component in the normal teaching. Observations showed that the teachers were able to incorporate the learning strategy training, but did so in a number of different ways and with rather varied acceptance from the students. This study illustrated the difficulty of taking a set of ideas from research and getting teachers to implement it: there is a *training* problem, because teachers usually need rather more than a couple of discussion sessions to change their ways of teaching, even for a limited period; and, more fundamentally, there is a *professional* problem, because the impetus for change so often comes (as in this case) from outside the teachers and their teaching programme rather than from within it. One can only speculate what the results might have been if the impetus to adopt strategy training had come from the teachers instead of from a group of research associates. O'Malley *et al.* maintain, correctly, that the locus of this experimentation has to be real classes with regular teachers, not imported 'experts' or researchers; but their execution of this policy left a problem which could well have biased their results seriously.

Teaching particular strategies

A small number of studies have attempted to obtain evaluative data on proposals for training students in strategies for particular skill areas, or indeed in particular strategies. Hosenfeld's training programme for reading has already been described. Also in reading, Carrell, Pharis, and Liberto (1989) reported a study in which two 'metacognitive' strategies for reading were compared with each other, and with a control. The two metacognitive strategies were a technique called (1) Semantic Mapping and another called (2) the Experience–Text Relationship method (ETR). In Semantic Mapping, the expected central categories of the argument and their inter-relations are sketched out graphically before reading the text, and again after the actual text has been read through; the two are then compared. In this sense it is a 'technical aid': students are taught to organize their thoughts and then their interpretation of the text in a kind of labelled diagram. Several advantages are claimed for this technique: students are able to anticipate what might be coming, prepare likely vocabulary, and then compare their expectation with the actual text. It is essentially a way of organizing background knowledge and comparing expectations with textual reality. In ETR, a dialogue is established between teacher and student first about the student's own background knowledge relevant to the topic, second about the text, usually read in sections, and third about the relationship between student experience and information contained in the new text.

Needless to say, both these techniques may be viewed both as student strategies and as teaching techniques; as the latter, they are quite familiar from many modern reading textbooks under the heading of 'pre-text exercises'. The two are similar, in that they both emphasize pre-reading review and post-reading comparison; they are different in so far as Semantic Mapping demands a visual product – a translation or channel conversion into diagram form; while ETR requires a particular kind of non-directive teacher questioning, and there is no visual product.

Carrell and her co-workers found that students using either of these techniques improved compared to the control group, but that improve-ment occurred on different measures of reading. Thus, multiple-choice questions on the text revealed no differences between the two treatments and the control – presumably the measurement itself was not sensitive enough. Open-ended questions favoured both treatment groups over the control group; a semantic map task with pre-set gaps like a Cloze favoured the ETR group; and an open-ended semantic map favoured the Semantic Mapping group. Furthermore, improvements associated with these tech-niques were closely related to individual differences in preferred learning styles, as reported on a questionnaire. So, in sum, this study successfully demonstrated that metacognitive techniques work, but that the improve-ment is not universal, only noticeable on certain measures of comprehen-sion, and that it is strongly determined by students' individual preferences for learning style. Carrell et al.'s study was conducted with students at uni-versity following ESL courses, and was embedded in their normal instruc-tion. However, the period of the study training only extended over a few days, and there was not a large number of students, so – as the authors fully recognize – the evidence cannot support sweeping generalizations.

A study by Kern (1988; 1989) used various think-aloud tasks and other measures to investigate strategy training in learning words in context among a group of university students of French. He found that strategies for learning discourse meaning were more effective than those for word or phrase level among these students, and that strategy training was more effective with the lower-ability students than with those of medium or high ability. Strategies were also more useful when combined with other strategies. These results echo themes we have already encountered: top-down and bottom-up strategies, here favouring the top-down type; the relationship of strategy use with proficiency in the language, here favouring the lower-proficiency ranges; and combinations of strategies being more effective than single-strategy use.

Summary and conclusions

It is clear that, although learning strategies, learners' beliefs and 'theories in action', and strategy training are very important elements in the teaching–learning process, great care has to be exercised in moving from a descriptive and taxonomic position to an interventionist one. That is to say, finding out what students are actually doing, and why, and in what circumstances and stage of learning, holds considerable promise for explaining the process of learning. Intervening in that process by selecting particular strategies or batteries of strategies for teaching is by contrast fraught with dangers, which are associated with the preparation of the teachers, the method of teaching, the cultural background of the students, and with many variables such as proficiency, learning style, and the language-learning task with which strategy use interacts.

Furthermore, we have seen that doing 'experiments' to evaluate the intervention has only been partially successful:

- Disrupting regular classes to assign students randomly to treatment group and control group removes the experiment from one of the crucial questions – does the treatment work in ordinary classes taught by regular teachers?
- Improvements in language proficiency caused by strategy training are relatively weak and only show up on certain kinds of measures.
- Cultural preferences in learning behaviours may be stronger than any strategy teaching effect.
- Improvements in proficiency may be better with lower-proficiency students.
- Strategy use and motivation to learn are closely associated, so measures of attitudinal differences are also needed.

- None of the studies so far to hand have looked at the maintenance of strategy use over time.
- In general, the introduction of innovation by researchers rather than teachers may not lead to the desired result anyway.

In the next chapter we turn to implications of research on strategies for test-taking, and to some important issues for classroom teaching raised by this survey of the state of knowledge about the strategies of the skilled and the unskilled learner.

6

Skills and strategies in test taking

Introduction

Whereas so far in this book skills for language using and language learning have been regarded in a positive light, and there has been a general assumption that discovering their nature enriches our knowledge and improves learning, this chapter plays a somewhat different tune. For if being a skilled language learner is a desirable quality, leading to success and the avoidance of frustration, being a skilled language test taker – while still undeniably a very useful thing to be – implies subversion of the purpose of language tests, which is to provide a true reflection of proficiency, and at worst calls into question the basis of our judgements about the truth of what language tests measure. This chapter will explore what is meant by test-taking strategies and their implications for the design of tests and test items. Further issues to be raised are the notion of construct validity, and the possibility of test formats reflecting the view of language competence which includes a component of strategic competence.

Tests are not natural language use

One of the most obvious difficulties is that most, if not all, test item types and formats are to some extent unnatural. Nobody uses multiple choice in natural language use. Word deletion as in a Cloze test is analogous to interruptions of intelligibility on a bad telephone line, but is hardly the norm. One is not normally quizzed after reading a book or listening to the news. The more recent moves towards authenticity of task within tests, to be seen in, for example, the Oxford Delegacy of Local Examinations test of general English, specific purposes tests such as the Cambridge English for Business and Industry Test, and the now withdrawn Test of English for Educational Purposes, demonstrate a recognition of this unnaturalness and a willingness on the part of testers to adopt more 'direct' or 'job-sample' item types. However, no such steps can remove the basic contrast between using a language for normal communicative purposes and using a language to demonstrate proficiency. Van Lier (1989), in a paper with an amusing title and a very serious message, has documented how far removed even the straightforward Oral Proficiency Interview is from the ordinary conversation it is supposed to represent. Although van Lier's criticisms are specifically derived from experience in the Inter-Agency Roundtable format (a development of the Foreign Service Institute's Oral Proficiency Interview), the general points he makes are probably true as well of the more structured formats of tests like the International English Language Testing Service (IELTS) (British Council/University of Cambridge Local Examinations Syndicate – UCLES) and the Spoken English for Industry and Commerce Test offered by the London Chamber of Commerce and Industry. Work has to be done on these, and even newer formats such as the Cambridge Advanced English or the Certificates in Communicative Skills in English have hardly figured in the literature so far at all.

Test makers' concerns have rightly been with rectifying the serious flaws their products contain in terms of traditional validity and reliability as measuring instruments. However, this newer concern with task authenticity leads one inevitably to question many of the assumptions of older and well-understood item types and, further, to open up the apparently orderly world of testing to the seeming disorder of theorizing about the way learners behave and the ways in which learners perform language tasks.

It is not necessarily the case that unnatural language use can give no estimation of likely proficiency: evidently, there are many tests whose ability to give an estimate of a true score or true level of proficiency is fairly good. This can be documented by traditional means, such as counting whether the order of proficiency in which the test puts the learners is more or less matched by the order of proficiency in which a standard test puts them, or by the distribution of success and failure on another task – first-year or preliminary results in an academic subject in the case of academic-purpose tests – so-called concurrent or predictive validity. Similarly, tests can be compared with themselves in various ways to estimate their consistency of returning the same score for the same individual, thus establishing the average 'error' score in the test, which gives an indication of the fairness of the test scores, traditionally called reliability. Sophisticated devices exist for checking out test formats in this way, and the argument that a statistically valid and reliable test, despite using indirect formats and therefore unnatural samples of language use, can be a valuable instrument has been familiar for many years. However, it is evident from the foregoing chapters that conceptions of what learners actually do when faced with language use and language-learning problems have been changing radically, and the testing world has not been exempt from this atmosphere of development.

Being a skilled test taker

There has always been controversy about the extent to which tests measure the ability to take tests, rather than the underlying proficiency of which the test is purportedly a sample. This ability is sometimes called being test-wise, i.e. having some ingenuity, knowledge, or strategy to outwit the tester and find the right answer from clues in the test format rather than from actual knowledge of the language or skill in language use. In this sense, being a skilled test taker means getting marks on the test which over-estimate the true proficiency level. On the other hand, because many test item types are only indirect representations of ordinary language use, a candidate may fail to perform up to his or her true proficiency level because of confusion or unfamiliarity with the test format itself. There are in fact two different problems here: one of *validity* – just what is the test measuring? (language proficiency or test taking skill) – and *reliability* – how well does it measure it? (consistency and independence).

These problems have several very immediate practical effects. One is the number of features to be built into tests themselves to circumvent the ingenious test taker, such as randomization of position of correct answer in multiple-choice recognition items, evenness of length of alternatives, randomization of the order of comprehension questions, to thwart guessing and educated guessing. Another is the decision whether or not to allow specimen papers to be available for practice. The TOEFL test, perhaps the most widely used multiple-choice question test in the world, has always provided these, and there are many sets of practice materials, including some produced by the Educational Testing service itself, who are responsible for the TOEFL. The UCLES First Certificate in English has also generated many sets of practice materials, and to a lesser extent this is true of other less popular published standardized tests. It would indeed be foolish to attempt one of these tests without knowing what it is like, and it is arguable that fairness can be satisfied by all potential candidates receiving the same prior knowledge of test format and rubrics. By contrast, the UCLES/British Council ELTS adopted for some years the policy of not releasing specimen papers, merely descriptions of the test tasks, on the argument that it was not particularly important for candidates to know how to pass the test, rather that they be able to perform successfully in the target-language use situation (surviving as a student in a British university) for which the test was designed as a predictor.

The choice is real: the thwarting of bias of test results towards the skilled test taker either by making access to the nature of the test equal, by allowing test-taking training, or by encouraging concentration on the target language use by concealing details of the item types and therefore disallowing test-taking training. In the event, the ELTS policy was seen to be unfair in itself and, in common with general UCLES policy, specimen tests were released, and this has continued through the 1990 revision and development of the IELTS (Alderson and Clapham, 1992). In what follows, we shall see what can be discovered about the nature of this test-taking skill.

What do tests measure?

The usual ways of establishing what a test measures are by analysing its content in terms of language items and skills, in relation to a syllabus or a needs analysis, and/or by observing how scores on it relate to other scores such as other language tests, or performance measures such as academic assessments or other professional appraisals. In a sense, both of these are different examples of what has become known as construct validity: the true nature of the proficiency involved is a theoretical construct, and the test reflects that theoretical construct. Thus, analysis of content reveals, for example, the selection of grammatical constructions, vocabulary items, cohesive devices, intelligibility, identification of meaning, inference from context, and so on, on the assumption that language proficiency consists of knowing these facts about the language and being able to perform in it. By the same token, statistical analysis reveals the relationships that exist between test scores and other traits, relationships that may or may not fit in with the test maker's theoretical construct of what the test is about. There is always the danger that what a test seems to be measuring is not what actually makes the students score the way they do: the results may be due to something else. A case in point is the fate of Cloze technique. For many years it was thought that this tapped a peculiarly linguistic quality, the use of the natural redundancy in language in terms of communicative efficiency. (Ability to make sense of a degraded text – one with words or bits of words unreadable or blanked out – seems to vary with knowledge of the language.) However, careful work by Hansen and Stansfield (1981) showed that ability on Cloze tests is heavily contaminated by an intellectual or cognitive variable, field independence, and does not directly reflect linguistic proficiency.

The problem takes on an added dimension of uncertainty when one considers tests of language skill use and, in general, tasks requiring integration of several linguistic features and levels, as in reading and listening comprehension, writing, and oral proficiency, as compared with tests of knowledge of grammar, vocabulary, sound patterns, stress, and intonation. Skill tests can only be validated against some specification of the skill: a theoretical construct. Within the testing world such skill specifications are becoming more and more widely used: for example, the statements of skills and requirements at different levels used for the development of the Royal Society of Arts Communicative Use of English Test, and subsequently its descendant, the Certificates in Communicative Skills in English. The

following is the statement for the reading skill: 'Such a specification represents an operational definition of the tester maker's construct of reading
skill.'

At this point two questions arise. First, how can an evaluator determine
whether the specified terms in the construct are true of test takers' behaviour? In other words, how well does the test actually measure what it is
supposed to measure? Second, how good a theory of reading (or whatever)
is the tester's construct? In other words, how well does the tester's construct match developments in theorizing about the skill involved outside
testing? Recently several authorities have suggested that one way of
answering these questions is to look at the strategies of test takers using the
think-aloud method. On the first question, there are many unobservables
which can only be estimated, but as we have seen in the chapter on receptive skills in particular, there is much information to be gained from
various kinds of soft evidence, particularly think-aloud protocols and questionnaires; on the second, it is also evident that modern theorizing about
language skills has been taking progressively greater and more sophisticated account of what learners tell us in verbal protocols, and as a conse-
quence the testing world cannot ignore this. We have already seen one
example which might be considered as a testing example. Aslanian's work
(1985; see Chapter 3) used a gap-filling task reminiscent of Cloze procedure as a prompt for discussion of the learner's comprehension. He
found a rather confused picture: his learners had a very hazy idea of how to
relate general context to identification of particular words, and one of his
learners, who appeared to be fairly proficient, demonstrated increasing
confusion as she continued to discuss the solution of the comprehension
problem. His data suggest that using gap-filling as a measure of an important aspect of comprehension (use of context) may be invalid.

Importance of tests

Tests are traditionally thought of as contributing to two kinds of decision
in language-learning programmes: the *measurement of proficiency*, i.e. establishing the standard a learner has reached on some set of criteria, whether
in comparison with other learners or on some absolute scale, and the *evaluation of teaching programmes*, in which one – but only one – criterion is
whether the programme has worked in the simple sense that the learners
have learnt something. There is also a more complex issue concerning the
possibility that what people are going to be tested on is sometimes seen as a
determinant of syllabus content and how they will be taught, or 'washback'. These cannot be purely mechanistic exercises, however, since a test
score still requires interpretation before decisions can be made on the basis
of it, and the function of washback is partly a matter of policy. In both of

these areas, it can be argued that we need to know more about how test takers approach the task and the strategies they use.

Proficiency measurement

In this first area there are two aspects of concern to us here. One is that there is a strong thread running through work on skills and strategies which argues, with Canale and Swain (1980) and Bialystok (1990), that an element of proficiency is 'strategic competence': that language-getting and language-using strategies are not simply a means to an end but an integral part of the definition of proficiency. That is to say, the notion of strategic competence presupposes that part of being a good language learner and a good language user is the possession of an appropriate range of strategies for solving the linguistic problems that a language-learning career throws up. If that is the case (and it is, of course, a controversial position), then not only do we need to know what testees do when they take tests in order to evaluate the test itself, but we also need to know how to test the learners' ability to use appropriate strategies. The other aspect of concern, related to the first, arises out of the notion of criterion referencing. If the interpretation of a test score is derived from a specification of a criterion performance, as in tests that use guidelines such as the Inter-Agency Guidelines (the former FSI scale) or the English Speaking Union Framework Yardsticks (Carroll and West, 1989), then there are important aspects of that criterial proficiency which involve strategic behaviour: compensatory strategies in production tests, performance strategies in skill tests, and social/affective strategies, particularly in oral interviews. This is because a criterion-referenced interpretation, although the scores may be expressed as a number, is essentially a qualitative judgement.

Programme evaluation

In this second area it is patent that how a student behaves in a test situation allows the programme designer and the student to assess the value of the preparation. There are many other aspects of programme evaluation, of course: test scores are only one of several indicators of how a programme is performing, along with attrition rate, resource economy, teaching quality, participants' feelings, quality assessment and control, and so on. However, it will always be the case that courses that prepare students to be successful on tests will be more highly valued than courses which fail to do so. The argument here is concerned with the quality of that success, and the extent to which the measurement of success plays a part in evaluating the processes of delivery of the course by the institution and the take-up of course content by the students. On the more restricted issue of washback, there is, as we shall see, some controversy about the power of test content and format to determine syllabus content and teaching methods, at least without concurrent changes in materials and teacher-training methods. However, if test-taking strategies can be taught, it would be surprising if they were not taught; if language-using strategies were tested, it would be surprising if they were not taught. For both, the problem is identifying what is justifiable.

In the following section, we shall present what empirical work has been done to investigate these problems by doing protocol analyses of test takers taking tests.

What test takers do: test-taking strategies

Cohen (1984) reports a number of small-scale investigations which aimed at finding out what candidates report as they try to solve various types of test item, what they pay attention to, and how they arrive at the right answer. It was exploratory and informal work; so no firm conclusions can be drawn. However, it opened up an area of research which has since produced a number of well-controlled and sophisticated studies. A general problem was the difficulty of obtaining authentic data from test situations on which nothing depended, and another was that most of these studies did not employ the normal time span of tests. In both Cloze and multiple-choice reading tests, it was clear that the majority of test takers ignored the explicit instructions in the rubric about how to perform the test. Takers did not read the whole Cloze passage through before attempting to fill in the gaps; takers tried to read the questions before the text in the multiple-choice, or read a portion of text and tried to find a question about it. Both of these behaviours are characteristic of test taking, not of reading in a non-test situation; whether they are motivated by skill or experience or anxiety to get started on producing answers is not clear. (Anxiety was greater with the Cloze passages.)

In the Cloze situation, different strategies were associated with proficiency: when they did not know how to complete a gap, poor scorers were reluctant to guess from context and used translation, while high scorers guessed from the immediate context.

In the multiple-choice reading tests, a number of strategies were found which enabled the reader to get the right answer without actually knowing it from internal linguistic evidence. Surface matching of test item stem and reading passage, or clues even in the stem itself which matched with one of the options, allowed students to get the right answer for the wrong reasons. Cohen quotes one study where students were given the multiple-choice questions without the passage they were based on (Israel, 1982 cited by Cohen, 1984). These were four-choice items (correct answer and three distractors), so the chance score would have been 25 per cent, but both advanced and intermediate students scored nearly twice as well as chance would predict (49 and 41 per cent respectively), so they were using internal evidence rather than a random ticking procedure.

In some cases, with a text, students used internal evidence and inappropriate background knowledge to make inferences leading to the wrong answer – as in the following example (Cohen, 1984: 76):

> most dollars are earned in the fishing industry. . . . In spite of the fact that there are resources other than fish, such as timber in the forests of the foothills, agriculture on the upland plateaus, and, of course, oil, these latter are highly underdeveloped.

Question:
4. The most highly developed industry in Filanthropia is
(a) oil
(b) fishing
(c) timber
(d) none of the above

A student who chose 'oil' had reasoned that only oil would be highly developed, reading 'developed' in the technological sense. This procedure is also characteristic of ordinary unskilled reading.

Another study, this time of multiple-choice questions embedded in a continuous reading passage, was conducted Dollerup, Glahn, and Hansen (1982). They were interested also in how their Danish students (first-year college and final-year school students) processed these items. They isolated two broad strategies, called by them 'mainline reading', where the student uses the central idea of the passage as a point of reference for solving the individual questions, and 'fragmented reading', where the questions themselves acted as the focus for the activity. It would be tempting to suggest that mainline reading equates with fairly normal reading, whereas fragmented reading is a response to a particular kind of text, one interspersed with multiple-choice questions, i.e. a test. The authors comment that both 'styles' of reading were used by the same readers at different points, and this is consistent with many of the studies of the reading skill itself.

Dollerup *et al.* also gathered data on how their test takers solved the problem of decoding unfamiliar words, whether the correct answer or the distractors. There was considerable use of approximation – the belief that *hesitant* was cognate with Danish *haste* and therefore meant 'hasten'; translation; use of background knowledge; and others. The authors point out that these strategies are just as likely to lead to the correct answer as not. They also refer to common sense, but their example is more of a rigid belief that, in a passage about a strike, everything must be about not working, whereas their text was actually about a small cadre of volunteers who, in the 1974 miners' strike in Britain, kept working in the pits to keep them usable after the strike (Dollerup *et al.*, 1982: 95, 97):

Volunteer miners kept coal mines safe. Voluntary safety work

[21.1] carried out
[21.2] obstructed
[21.3] neglected

by miners during their strike in 1974 meant that all coal mines could resume production when the strike ended. After the previous strike 25 out of about 800 coal mines were lost, but this time cooperation between miners and management ensured that the pits were

[22.1] operating
[22.2] kept safe
[22.3] closed

during the strike. In addition to deputies and inspectors, who reported for duty each day, many miners

[23.1] were forced
[23.2] refused
[23.3] volunteered

to help in taking safety measures with their Union's approval . . .

One student's report: '[21.3] I pick 3 because they refuse to work during the strike; [22.3] "closed", because the mine must be closed during the strike. Nobody wants to work. [23.2] They refuse to work. When the majority refuses to work, the individual worker does so, too.'

Both these two exploratory studies attempt to draw a distinction between what students do in order to solve the test item problem – test-taking strategies – and what they might do normally in order to read a text – reading strategies – comparing the two to see in an informal and unquantifiable way what kind of overlap there might be between them. Not surprisingly, they conclude that some activities – for example fragmented reading – are particularly associated with test taking, and some might occur in both situations.

Part of a much more thoroughgoing study by Nevo (1989) on multiple-choice test-taking strategies concerned the use of what he calls 'non-contributory' strategies. These were strategies that he, by a decision process not explained in his paper, decided would not lead to correct answers. They were:

- guessing
- choosing the exception
- length
- location
- matching alternative with stem
- matching alternative with text.

These are in contrast with the 'contributory' strategies which are more like the reading strategies found in studies of reading, and which we shall discuss in the next section. Nevo found that, not surprisingly, significantly more use was made by his subjects in their second language (French) of these non-contributory strategies than in doing the reading text in their first language (Hebrew), and also that, even in the second language, significantly more use was made of the contributory strategies than of the non-contributory. Thus, performing in a second language – at least at this level – encourages greater use of strategies that refer to the physical format of the test items, which perhaps indicates a degree of 'test-wiseness'; but students nevertheless use 'reading' strategies to find the answers the clear majority of the time. Of these 'test-wise' strategies, referring to the format of the test items, by far the most frequent was 'guessing', defined as 'blind guessing not based on any particular rationale'. This was some three to four times as frequent in L2 as in L1. Of the others, only 'matching alternative with text' was used in any considerable frequency, and then more often in L1 than in L2. Such matching at least requires consideration of the text as well as the test item, and therefore might be considered a kind of hybrid between Nevo's two broad categories of strategy.

Presumably the greater use of 'non-contributory' test-taking strategies in L2 is a result of the greater uncertainty the candidates have that more conventional sources of information will lead to the correct answer. However, it is noteworthy in Nevo's results on this point that the frequency of these kinds of strategies in L1 is but a tenth of that of contributory strategies, and this proportion rises to one-third in L2. It remains to be seen, of course, whether the 'contributory' strategies on which the students spend most of their time bear any kind of close relationship to the sort of reading strategies and styles they report when engaged on reading for purposes other than being tested. It is this issue of whether reading tests measure reading to which we now turn.

Construct validity

A test, part of a test, or a testing technique, is said to have construct validity if it can be demonstrated that it measures just the ability which it is supposed to measure. The word 'construct' refers to any underlying ability (or trait) which is hypothesized in a theory of language ability. (Hughes, 1989: 26)

Thus Hughes begins his discussion of construct validity, and traditional means of establishing this have included statistical comparisons of the degree of similarity and difference between scores on tests hypothesized to tap relevant and irrelevant subskills – the process of convergent and divergent validation.

For various reasons, researchers are turning to other ways of pursuing this goal. One fairly simple way of doing this is to compare the strategies mentioned in the test situation with those mentioned in non-test situations. The 'contributory' strategies of Nevo's research (1989) with multiple-choice test items and the strategies isolated by Dollerup *et al.* are a case in point. Nevo's reading strategies are presented here in order of frequency of use. The orders in L1 and L2 were approximately the same:

1. *returning to the passage:* returning to the text to look for the correct answer, after reading the questions and the multiple-choice alternatives
2. *clues in the text:* locating the area in the test that the question referred to and then looking for clues to that answer in that context
3. *elimination:* selecting an alternative because the others did not seem reasonable or understandable
4. *ceasing search at plausible choice:* reading the alternative choices until reaching one thought to be correct, not continuing to read the other choices
5. *background knowledge:* general knowledge outside the text called up by the reader in order to cope with the written material
6. *chronological order:* looking for the answer in chronological order in the passage
7. *key word:* arriving at an alternative because it had in it a word that appeared to be a key word in the text
8. *association:* selecting the alternative because it had a word in it that evoked an association with a word in the native language or in another language known by the reader.

Clearly, the difference between ordinary reading and doing a multiple-choice reading test is reflected in the number of these strategies that are closely (but not solely) tied with the traditional format of the test: a test taker will use a process of *elimination* to solve the puzzle of which alternative seems the most appropriate; *ceasing search of plausible choice* reflects the format of distractors, although the reason for ceasing is recognition of some kind of correspondence between the alternative and the text.

Comparing these strategies with those gleaned from studies of the reading process (see the list in Chapter 3), two conclusions are immediately obvious. First, there are far fewer strategies mentioned in the test or quasi-test situation; and second, those that are mentioned (other than those that involve only test-format information) do not manifest the range discovered in the studies of reading itself. One reason for the first observation is probably the difference in methods of data collection: both Nevo's and Dollerup *et al.*'s research asked about the test items, not about reading the passage itself, and furthermore, while Dollerup *et al.* gave a reasonably free interview for the respondents to discuss the experiences in, Nevo used a sixteen-point checklist of strategies which the respondents ticked off, as well as a verbal report. Since the task had to be completed in a certain time to preserve the authenticity of the test situation, it is not surprising that the respondents did not report using other strategies than those on the list prepared by the researchers.

The second observation concerning range or coverage may be a result of the first: but it is striking that in neither the more restricted research of Nevo nor the more open method of Dollerup *et al.* did any 'technical aids' or 'monitoring' strategies receive a mention. Though 'background knowledge', 'knowledge of the world', and 'chronological order' are mentioned, no other 'coherence-detecting moves' are mentioned in the test situation; similarly, using 'grammar' and possibly 'synonyms' (if they may be deemed to be similar to 'association') are the only 'clarification and simplification' moves. On this basis, then, one has to conclude that the strategies reported in studies on these two kinds of reading test bear only a weak relationship to the activities reported by readers in a non-test situation, and no hint is given of individual differences such as Block's (1986) 'integrators' and 'non-integrators' of text.

A different kind of test: work on the C-test

Work by Feldmann and Stemmer (1987) and Grotjahn (1987) has been directed at a new form of reduced redundancy test, a descendant of Cloze, called the C-test. Feldmann and Stemmer's title demonstrates the format:

> Thin____ aloud a____ retrospective da____ in C-t____ taking: diff____ languages – diff____ learners – sa____ approaches?

In short, a C-test demands exact word gap-filling by mutilating words in regular ways rather than by omitting words at regular intervals. They put their problem succinctly thus (p. 251):

> The current state of research on the C-test can be summarised as follows: the C-test is very economical and, above all, a highly reliable measurement instrument. However, what it measures, i.e. its construct validity, is, in our opinion, thus far quite unclear.

Accordingly, they used verbal protocols to try to find out how learners of various languages taking this new kind of test actually approached the task.

Their test takers' verbal reports (given on tape while doing the test, and in an interview afterwards) reveal a number of fascinating behaviours. Feldmann and Stemmer distinguished between general problem-solving and specific problem-solving, and further between automatic and non-automatic retrieval of the mutilated word.

One general decision which a test taker is faced with is whether to read the whole passage before tackling the test items or to proceed item by item. With the passage + question format, it is often assumed that takers will read the whole passage before tackling the questions; but they often do not, as was shown by Cohen. With the Cloze test, it is often part of the rubric, and is equally often ignored. With the C-test, only 5 per cent even tried to do this, but found that the great proportion of mutilations made them stop and go back to plough through the text word by word. Thus, C-tests do not involve the kind of 'skimming' or 'scanning' techniques so prevalent in studies of reading and teaching methodologies.

Feldmann and Stemmer also looked in detail at the non-automatic retrieval strategies, dividing these into recall and evaluation. A number of these are the same as have been demonstrated in studies of reading in non-test situations:

- *Recall by*
  structural analysis
  adding letters
  repetition
  past situation
  search for meaning
  external help
  substitution

- *Evaluation by*
  checking on meaning of item (translation, use of co-text)
  checking on form of item (analysis, translation, sound)
  other means.

Clearly some of these are 'bottom-up' and some 'top-down' strategies; but the majority concern word identification rather than passage comprehension. Background knowledge features, but none of their students referred to textual cohesion, frameworks, or other 'metacognitive' strategies. This is, of course, not surprising in a test that is constructed by mutilating individual words.

It is interesting that the C-test research reveals more overtly 'evaluative' strategies than the multiple-choice research, and this is probably because it refers to a reconstructive rather than a recognition task. However, the general picture of C-test taking in Feldmann and Stemmer's (and also in Grotjahn's 'exploratory-nomological') research is of finding words rather than of constructing meanings. This may be bad news for the C-test, but it strongly demonstrates the utility of verbal report methods in the evaluation of tests.

Multiple choice, verbal reports, and discrimination

The most thoroughgoing piece of research in construct validity in multiple-choice reading tests to date was performed by Anderson, Bachman, Perkins, and Cohen (1991). This involved Spanish native speakers enrolled in an ESL programme in the United States. The researchers aimed to measure the relationships between test takers' performance on the test, what they reported about their reading and test-taking strategies, and theoretical analyses of what the test was supposed to measure, i.e. the construct of reading skill. The importance of this study is that it collected both quantitative and qualitative data, and subjected it both to interpretive and to numerical analysis. Thus is can justifiably claim to be a 'triangulation' study. The most important findings of the study – apart from the fact that it was possible to perform it at all – were the insights about the relationship between particular strategy uses and discrimination, i.e. whether the use of certain strategies on certain item types was associated with good or poor reading as measured by the test, and what the test developers thought the test was supposed to be measuring. They drew up a list of forty-seven possible strategies using research studies of reading and of testing (including Nevo's), grouped into strategies for Supervising, Support, Paraphrase, Coherence, and Test-Taking. They only actually used data on the seventeen of the forty-seven strategies whose overall frequency of use was ten times or greater among their twenty-eight respondents, to eliminate undue bias from idiosyncratic responses. The seventeen were:

- Supervising
    3. stated failure to understand
    8. refer to lexical items
    11. respond affectively to text
- Support
    14. skim
    15. scan
- Paraphrase
    19. paraphrase
    21. extrapolate from information presented in text
- Coherence
    23. reread
    25. react to author's style
- Test-Taking
    30. guess
    32. select answer through elimination
    33. select answer through deductive reasoning
    34. match stem with item

35. select answer because stated in text
36. select answer based on understanding text
37. make reference to time
43. express uncertainty at correctness of answer.

From this list it is easy to see that eight of these strategies – half – are in the test-taking category. Another way of putting the same point is to say that half of the original category of test-taking strategies occur in the strategies used with frequency greater than ten times, but only between a third and a fifth of any other category achieves such a frequency.

They also classified the test items according to what the test developers themselves thought they were testing:

● understanding the main idea
● understanding a direct statement
● making an inference.

They found that certain strategies were used significantly more often on certain kinds of question than on others, implying that the categories of question had a reality in terms of how the takers behaved in answering them.

The authors considered that the most important findings concerned the combination of all three sources of information – verbal reports, item characteristics, and question classification. Strategy 37, 'making reference to time', when looked at from these three points of view, indicates that when students are coping with direct statement-type questions that actually discriminate well between good and poor readers, they do worry about the time allocation – not surprisingly!

'Stated failure to understand' (strategy 3) was most frequent on items that discriminated among good performers on the test, less frequent on easy items, and on items that simply discriminated between good and poor readers. It looks like an admission that students only make under test conditions on the most sensitive items.

'Paraphrasing' (strategy 19) was employed particularly with items of medium level of difficulty, and especially with understanding direct statements rather than inferences or the main idea.

'Guessing' (strategy 30) occurred especially with inference items and medium difficulty items – those that discriminate well between good and poor readers. This tallies with Nevo's finding that guessing was used more by good readers than poor ones.

'Matching stem with the previous portion of the text' (strategy 34) was used particularly with inference items, but less on the main ideas and direct statements, more often with items of medium difficulty. Test takers may here be trying to find answers in a text where the answer rather lies in a logical inference from the text.

Anderson *et al.* described their study as a pilot, as it certainly broke new ground. It raises a number of serious questions for construct validity, and shows a way (however complicated) of finding some of the answers. Further questions would be, for example:

1. How could a more sophisticated construct of reading be validated? After all, thirty of the strategies postulated were only reported fewer than ten times, indicating that they were unlikely candidates for a universal theory of reading in test situations; and the classification of items into main idea, direct statement, and inference, was remarkably crude.

2. From this research it would not be proper to conclude that those thirty strategies that appeared fewer than ten times each represent a conspicuous lack of construct validity, simply because we do not know if these student readers would have used them more if they had not been in a test situation. One would need to be able to show that the readers behaved significantly differently in the test and the ordinary reading situation to defend that conclusion. However, it seems a likely proposition.

3. Could this kind of study be performed with different kinds of item type, such as short-answer questions, Cloze, scrambled paragraphs, labelled diagrams, conceptual maps, summarizing, or speeded reading?

4. Could a similar kind of triangulation study be performed on tests of other skills such as listening, writing, or oral skills? Hamp-Lyons (1990) has already called for ethnographic research into writers' encounters with writing test questions. Buck (1991) has produced a think-aloud study of listening-test performance, which focused on short-answer questions, which are relatively rare in listening tests because of the timing problem. His results revealed a number of concerns, in particular with time management; inference questions ('higher-order questions'); response set (not using the inferences made in the composed answers); and the consistency through the answers of the interpretations constructed.

Problems with test-taking strategies and research

These studies raise numerous interesting problems, both issues of principle and issues of methodology, which will contribute further development in this growth area. Taking the issues of methodology first, there are at least the following questions that need to be decided when more research is contemplated along these lines:

1. Tests in the normal situation are timed. Research has to balance the need to preserve the authenticity of the test situation with the need to give respondents long enough to do more than just tick a prepared checklist and give their own responses. Moreover, information about test takers' strategies for coping with time pressures is itself needed, and both the Anderson and Buck studies made a start on this.

2. As with other think-aloud and verbal report data, a certain amount of training improves the quality of the data. However, we are entitled to query how valid information can be from a method of research that requires training of the respondents in observation and reporting, about a set of tasks which themselves require training (test-taking practice) designed to measure the result of training (learning to read, etc.).

3. There is reason to believe that the yield in terms of strategy use is dependent on item difficulty, from Anderson *et al.* (1991), Cohen (1984), and Nevo (1989). This constraint needs further investigation because item difficulty is obviously related to proficiency: we need more information on how readers of different levels process the same items.

4. Can one generalize to other test-taker populations?

5. What happens if the test 'counts'?

Conclusions

There are, lastly, a number of interesting issues of principle, with which I shall conclude.

1. The research to date has had relatively limited coverage of skills and test item types. We do not know yet what test takers do in all sorts of item types which are different to the rather traditional ones (with the exception of the novel C-test). In particular, test makers are now developing a whole range of new item types to meet the new certification challenges such as test of communication skills, test of specific-purpose language using authentic materials (e.g. the Cambridge English for Industry and Business Test, the Oxford Industry and Business English Certificate, the London Chamber of Commerce and Industry's Spoken English for Industry and Commerce), tests administered via video (the British Council/BBC English Video Test) which make in some cases strong claims about task authenticity.

2. Are strategies always strategies? As with the discussion about strategies and skills in non-test situations, there is only a loose classification available, and it is not certain that every piece of research that invokes the notion is using it in the same sense. Strategies tend to be thought of as deliberate, conscious, cognitive, and reportable. Bialystok (1990) demonstrates that at least for communication strategies, each of these features can be refuted. It is prima facie strange that a reaction such as 'stated failure to understand' should be counted as a strategy for solving a reading problem or a test item!

3. In accordance with the shift from preoccupation with product to interest in process that this approach implies, test makers are beginning to look at the possibilities of testing not simply the language skill but the skilled language user – the skilled reader, the skilled talker, the skilled listener, the skilled writer. As more information on the components of

these skills becomes available, so test makers can find appropriate means to test for them. However, there are problems: in the Examiner's report on the first year of operation of the Cambridge Certificate of Advanced English, there is a mention that students were asking for more time to complete a reading test which was timed deliberately to encourage skim-reading and scan-reading, two of the most obvious reading strategies considered in the literature. Test takers can thwart such moves, either by inertia or more reasonably by adopting more deliberate strategies than the test maker intended.

4. Test formats and test content, it is often argued, exert influence on teaching. This is usually called 'washback'. Studies of teaching a strategic approach and specific strategies for the various skills have met with only mixed success (O'Malley and Chamot, 1990; Wenden, 1987), and in some cases the results constitute a warning (Politzer and McGroarty, 1985). One needs to be careful that the washback effect from tests with an avowed aim of testing strategic behaviour, if developed, is not allowed to bias learners in ways that are not desirable. We do not want to create a new breed of skilled test takers – rather a generation of good learners who can demonstrate their knowledge and skills in valid language tests. Alderson and Wall (1993) have in any case cast doubt on the strength of washback in various language programmes; but in many places tests are still used as controlling devices over syllabuses and teaching methods.

7

Strategies and skills in the classroom

Introduction

A book about aspects of students' learning and language-using activities should not fall into the trap of suggesting or, even worse, prescribing what teachers should or should not do in classrooms. The usefulness of information on learning various language skills is best seen as explanatory and consultative, not decisive. Too often in the history of applied linguistics, researchers, theorists, and materials developers have taken investigatory results as the starting-point and justification for prescriptions of method where either the new knowledge concerned has been quickly seen as invalid or illusory, or rigid application of the method so developed has led to widespread disillusion and the rejection of the innovation. If there is scope for methodological innovation in the literature on skills and strategies in learning languages, then it is worth devising ways of both evaluating and maintaining those innovations.

This chapter will therefore not develop detailed prescriptions for teaching on the basis of implications of the material so far discussed, but will instead look at four issues for the classroom which, to this writer, seem to arise from the idea of becoming a skilled learner and a skilled language user.

Strategic teaching

First we shall review, in the light of the remarks above concerning innovation, the suggestions put forward for 'strategic teaching'.

The syllabus

The idea of a syllabus as an externally imposed learning plan is seriously challenged by the view that learners have their own learning agendas.

The skilled classroom learner

If we can get learners to reveal their learning processes and strategies in language skill areas and tests, then we can also get them to reveal their reactions to the techniques which are used to teach them, and perhaps glimpse their processing of these. A skilled language learner possesses skill in coping not only with problems of language but with the context of learning – and for large numbers of learners this context is the classroom.

Evaluation

The chapter concludes by commenting on the use of process information in evaluation.

Implications for classroom management and materials design

Incorporation and implication

Several proposals already exist, as sets of teaching materials, for the incorporation of strategic teaching. O'Malley and Chamot describe the 'Cognitive Academic Language Learning Approach' in several publications (e.g. 1990), and have attempted to assess its success. The CALLA system is designed to work through content-based ESL teaching; it employs the three-way classification of learning strategies discussed in Chapter 5 (metacognitive, cognitive, and social-affective), and in general consists of five phases (O'Malley and Chamot, 1990: 158):

1. *preparation*: develop student awareness of different strategies
2. *presentation*: develop student knowledge about strategies
3. *practice*: develop student skills in using strategies for academic learning
4. *evaluation*: develop student ability to evaluate their own strategy use
5. *expansion*: develop transfer of strategies to new tasks.

At each stage there is a clear mix of student self-revelation and teacher input.

O'Malley and Chamot's approach was developed out of the research experience with learning-strategy training, in experiments and observations with strategy use, reported in O'Malley *et al.* (1987; 1989*a*, *b*) and O'Malley and Chamot (1990). The learning-strategy teaching package itself does not seem to have been evaluated to date in any formal way. O'Malley and Chamot comment, on the basis of their experience in running workshops with teachers on the approach, that it 'requires a high level of teacher knowledge and skill'. They claim it is of benefit in many different kinds of programme for students of different levels with different learning purposes. There is as yet, however, as with other systems to be described briefly below, no independent evaluation of these claims of effectiveness and versatility.

Another set of materials that has been in use for about the same time is that of Ellis and Sinclair (1989). They divide their approach into three rather broad groups of strategies:

1. personal strategies (discovery of the students' preferred styles)
2. risk-taking strategies (paraphrase, rule-invention, prediction, rehearsing talk, revising compositions)
3. organization strategies – for resources, materials, and time.

Ellis and Sinclair present a whole range of activities designed to help learners discover and elaborate their strategic potential and organize the language, the learning material, and the time available for themselves. It is conceived as a separate learning activity from the actual language learning, though it may be both preparatory to and concurrent with the language lessons. It is not directly related to the content base of the language lessons, as is the O'Malley and Chamot proposal.

A third set of instructional materials arises from and was constructed for the Australian Migrant English Program (AMEP). Willing (1989) produced these materials to aid learners enrolled in this large-scale federal programme for Australian citizens who were not native speakers of English to gain sufficient English to participate in economic, social, and cultural life. The organization of these materials follows a similar pattern all the way through: the particular strategy is explored and example activities for each one are worked through. The Willing materials are for class use, with a set of activity worksheets on each of the strategies, and a teacher's guide to explain the concepts involved and the aim of each activity. Willing divides the material thus:

Part 1. Managing the learning process
1. having an understanding of your own language learning
2. making learning plans
3. managing communicative situations
4. practising
5. monitoring and evaluating

Part 2. Managing information
6. selectively attending
7. associating
8. categorizing
9. pattern learning
10. inferencing.

The activities are graded, with suitable suggestions in each strategy for beginner, post-beginner, intermediate, post-intermediate, and advanced learners. Willing makes the point that one important aim of these materials is to make the learners more independent, and therefore less likely to see the language classes themselves as the only source or locus of language learning: having learned these strategies in class, so it is argued, the students can make greater use of learning opportunities in the English-speaking culture, both inside and outside their home. This aim is in a sense a response to the situation Willing (1985) found in a study of learning-style preferences among AMEP students in which the top four questions (those that were marked as 'best' by the greatest number of people) related directly to classroom activities, and indeed to a distinct dependence on the teacher (percentage figures in brackets):

Q20 I like to practise the sounds and the pronunciation   (62)
Q11 I like the teacher to tell me all my mistakes   (61)
Q4   In class, I like to learn by conversations   (55)
Q8   I like the teacher to explain everything to us   (54)

Willing performed several statistical analyses of these questionnaire results, which are beyond the scope of this discussion, and they demonstrated the existence of recognizable individual differences in his large sample of adult learners. Willing's materials also conflate a number of contrasts in the discussion of strategies, for deliberate pedagogic reasons. For example, some of his strategy materials relate more to conscious awareness, some to making skills more automatic, some to specific language skills, and some to language material and other kinds of content.

These three sets of formally produced and trialled materials, from three different parts of the English-speaking world, demonstrate that there is both a need and ways of satisfying that need for learner-centred material designed to open up the learning task for the learners. All three share, in different ways, the feature noted many years ago by Hosenfeld, of starting where the learners are and eliciting from them their own beliefs, preconceptions, and experience, before introducing changes and procedures based on professional analysis of the language-use problems and of other language learners' successes.

Incorporation in particular skills areas

In more modest vein, proposals have been developed for preparing students to face the kinds of problem that occur in particular skill areas. A clear example is the popular work on the writing process outlined in Chapter 3. Many of the facets of student writing noted there do not feature in the macro-approaches outlined in the previous section, but they have been incorporated in instructional schemes for approaching the writing task. One set of materials arising directly out of writing process research is Arndt and White's (1991) 'Process Writing'. In this text, students are given exercises to orient them to the organic task of producing text by considering planning tasks, topic orientation tasks, editing and revising tasks, and so on. Another example is Cohen's work on vocabulary learning (1992). Floyd's 'Study Reading' (1988) deliberately introduces the student to texts about the reading process – for example varying the reading rate, flexibility, and prediction, in an attempt to exercise the students' language study strategies and extend them to other study situations.

Since one of the results of the strategy discovery research is that strategy use can vary greatly between individuals, there is a danger that incorporating particular strategies, however sensible they are, into teaching texts can constrain rather than extend the learner's range. Consequently, many (but not all) materials for introducing a strategic approach concentrate on discovering the learner's beliefs and preferential modes of action and adapting them, rather than prescribing remedies.

Not surprisingly, given the scarcity of empirical studies of listening strategies, there are currently no sets of materials for teaching strategic listening based on empirical work. However, several listening courses present exercises focused on areas such as selective attention for linguistic features, top-down inferences using schematic knowledge, integrating information from different parts of the text, using background knowledge, and using co-text for interpreting unknown words (Anderson and Lynch, 1989; McDonough, 1978).

Implications for syllabus design

One of the currently most discussed principles in syllabus design is the task-based syllabus. This syllabus, essentially a grading system based not on the language system, communication needs, or accessibility of topics, but on tasks whose difficulty varies in manipulable ways, is especially interesting with regard to strategic behaviour. The reason is that the features that make some tasks more difficult than others and encourage different kinds of language input and output are features which learners have to cope with using various kinds of strategy. In this book we have already come across several examples: the difference in planning behaviour and cognitive load noted by Jones and Tetroe as between writing tasks involving completion of a passage with the beginning, or the end, given; the difference in amount of editing and revising performed by learners in producing compositions and in producing summaries. Crookes (1989) provides another example: giving an immediate spoken response to an information-gap task compared to having ten minutes' planning time. Crookes found that the planning time did not affect the accuracy of the language produced, but rather the variety of vocabulary and grammar chosen.

Kroll (1990*b*) found a similar result with different times allowed for writing tasks. Planning time built into a task is only one possible variable, and Skehan (1992) discusses evidence concerning several variables in task design in relation to their effect on learning behaviour and what, in his words, 'drives forward the language system' (1992: 202), such as:

- communicative stress
- number of participants
- size of linguistic resource
- background knowledge
- amount of pre-teaching in preparation for the task.

To those could be added the method of integration of elements of reception and production in the tasks. Skehan makes the point that, according to some pieces of research, an effort towards communication and interactional success may not contribute to overall growth in the learner's language system, but to fossilization of certain strategic solutions to the communicational and interactional problems encountered. In support of this argument, he quotes Schmidt's (1983) study of a Japanese learner of English (Wes) who clearly progressed in communication ability, but whose progress was mainly in the area of strategic and discourse competence, and much less in grammatical competence. If this evidence of the separate development of strategic and other kinds of linguistic competence was supported by other studies, then the role of intervention in some systematic way, perhaps through training in appropriate learning strategies (as contrasted with communication strategies) in a task-based syllabus, would be much clearer.

There is, at present, no generally accepted analytic framework or taxonomy for tasks to use as a reliable basis for syllabus design. There are, however, a number of proposals, from Long and Crookes (1986), Prabhu (1987), and Willis (1990). Empirical research is needed, including exploratory research in the think-aloud tradition, to discover how students cope with and respond to the interventions in the learning process which the design features of language-learning tasks represent. In other words, what do students do with the teaching techniques that teachers use with them? In the testing context, we have already seen how time management features as the object of coping strategies in language-testing situations, where there is stress of a different sort from communicative stress. This and other variables, such as those quoted by Skehan, need investigation in the rich atmosphere of the classroom.

Student views of the learning process

Empirical research on student behaviour and coping strategies need not wait upon the development of new syllabus proposals such as task-based learning. One of the most enduring mysteries in language-teaching research is what students actually do while attending language classes –

- how much attention they pay
- what to
- how they process the language environment
- what the significance of participation or apparent non-participation is
- in what ways they understand the procedures of the lesson
- what events retain significance for learning and why
- how the distribution of talk and interactional patterns affect them
- how they cope with the teacher's usual inconsistencies in error-correction behaviour
- what they value and do not value, etc.

In this section we shall look at empirical work on several aspects of student views: views arising from cultural misconceptions of the parameters of teaching, views about particular teaching techniques, views about the significance of classroom events for 'uptake', and typical behaviours of students in paying attention and processing feedback. In many cases we shall see that there is a wide degree of divergence between students' views and their teachers'.

Cultural tensions

It is almost a commonplace in discussion of teaching English for Academic Purposes for overseas students that much of the style of learning that such courses prepare students for is not only unfamiliar but contrary to styles they understand from their own educational experience. Two much-discussed examples (Bloor and Bloor, 1989; Ballard, 1984) are the notion of independent or autonomous learning and the notion of intellectual property. Many students from overseas do not immediately understand or relish the expectation that their success is largely their own responsibility and not that of, for example, their teachers. Connected with this is also a misconception of what academic success consists of – what is valued in another education system. Bloor and Bloor quote a student who is surprised at the role of written assessments in the British university she had entered because assessment in her previous academic career up to first-degree level was by multiple-choice questions, encouraging the development of a good memory for facts. The formal and implicit requirements of an academic essay in English were something for which she was quite unprepared. The notion of intellectual property underlies the different attitudes of staff and students to procedures such as acknowledgement of sources and the use of quotations: an essay consisting mainly of unacknowledged quotations is seen by staff in a university in the Western tradition as essentially a stolen good, sometimes incurring the wrath of the institution in formal charges of 'passing off the work of others as your own' or plagiarism, whereas to the student the quotations may be simply the best way of expressing the ideas involved because written by the creators of those ideas. These are familiar examples, and they concern people who have moved from one culture to study in another.

However, similar mismatches may occur in the home situation of the learners, when methodological innovation is imported that has been developed and trialled elsewhere. Maclennan (1987) has investigated student groups in Hong Kong and Macau, to establish their beliefs about good teacher and student behaviour. She was interested in comparing their attitudes with those described earlier by Maley (1983, cited by Maclennan, 1987) on the basis of his experience of mainland China. Using a questionnaire approach, Maclennan asked group members about their attitudes to good teaching, student autonomy, student contributions, literature, tests, and several other themes. She found that they:

- rated the quality of being 'well-trained and experienced' highest, contrasting in fact with the Mainland Chinese preference for 'knowing the language best' found by Maley
- preferred a teacher who 'graded all their work' rather then let them assess their own or their peers', revealing an antipathy to, or perhaps just a misunderstanding of, contemporary moves towards student autonomy
- wanted to listen to the teacher in class rather than work in pairs or talk to other students, demonstrating discomfort with the use of peers as resources for language and practice
- saw literature in the classroom as a way of gaining more knowledge about another culture rather than as material on which to develop their own critical judgement, revealing a preference for the acquisition of products rather than personal development.

Their attitudes to tests were more complex: they saw these by and large (but not unanimously) as essential and not used too often, and aiming at mastery of the language rather than just passing or failing. Maclennan comments that it is not easy to separate out the contribution of acquiescence – students guessing what the researcher's preferred answer is – from this sort of data. However, her results give an interesting clue to student reception or understanding of elements of the teaching techniques they are subject to, in a context where much of the training for language teachers and some of the language teachers themselves are imported from another (colonial) culture.

A perspective on this problem from people who have chosen to learn English in a different culture from their own is afforded by a study conducted among the transient population enrolled at private language schools in Britain by EFL Services Ltd in 1992. The method used was a 'focus group' discussion in English between a researcher and a group of volunteers from the school. The researcher, or 'moderator', had an agenda in the form of a sequence of topics about which to elicit opinions and the task of ensuring the free flow of conversation; the participants had their experiences to talk about. The groups ranged between three and ten participants, averaging six; being self-selecting, participation was, of course, not controlled for any variables like sex, age, or level of proficiency. This technique is used in market research, but not normally in psychological research. Two of the topic areas on which opinions were solicited from the groups were 'learning in Britain' and 'progress'.

Many participants commented that they knew that classroom life would be different from that in their own countries – after all, they had come to gain more chance of speaking:

> In Japan usually most of the teachers are Japanese. I think it's a problem ... I think they hardly speak English, they know grammar. I understood our teacher but I couldn't express myself in English because I wasn't used to speaking or listening. (1992, p. 63)

> The materials are more or less the same ... The same sort of things happen in the classroom. (1992, p. 7)

Some other students remarked on a welcome difference between an examination orientation and a personal investment orientation:

> There's no stress in England because in school you have to learn for exams and for marks. In England you have to learn for your own reasons and that's much more fun. (1992, p. 7)

However, some classroom activities were highlighted for criticism partly because they did not satisfy that personal (and financial) investment:

> Most people came to London because they want to work hard, they want to learn something. You waste so much time just understanding the game you have to play ... if the game is not successful it's just a waste of time and I paid too much. (1992, pp. 29–30)

Not all the opinions were anti-games, but the activity was seen as a high-risk venture: 'Good games are very good, bad games are very bad' (p. 30).

Perceptions of progress by this self-selecting group of customers were interestingly moderate, and this may be linked with the feeling expressed in the above quotation that a positive feature of this kind of learning situation was the lack of external assessment:

What progress?

In some cases considerable progress was felt to have been made. But for the majority the incontestable signs of success were less obvious. This did not appear to cause major disappointment. If anything was to blame, it was the short time available, the nature of the language learning in general, and English in particular, or the participant's own lack of application. Some participants would have appreciated a procedure which allowed them to measure their progress but it has to be said that such comments were usually prompted rather than volunteered. In general, progress was felt to have been modest but perfectly satisfactory. (p. 74)

One might have expected that a population of fee-paying customers might have felt dissatisfied without some tangible signs of return on their investment; but clearly here this does not seem to have been an issue. If it were, learner education in techniques of self-evaluation might be an appropriate development.

Student views of the classroom

Experience within the AMEP has been reported by Nunan (1988). One of the by-products of the shift from a more traditional school-based ELT provision to a learner-centred curriculum involving much more teacher mobility was a series of quite large-scale pieces of research into this student population; and on this topic teachers' views were also canvassed, enabling comparisons to be made. Alcorso and Kalantzis (1985, reported by Nunan, 1988) investigated the perceptions of students enrolled in the AMEP. Students on this programme were mainly adult and looking for English tuition outside normal public schooling, and from a variety of national and ethnic origins. A survey of them produced the following order of preference for activities, phrased as 'the most useful parts of a lesson' (Alcorso and Kalantzis, 1985, reported in Nunan, 1988: 90, table 6.3):

Activity	%
Grammar exercises	40
Structured class discussion/conversation	35
Copying written material, memorising, drill and repetition work	25
Listening activities using cassettes	20
Reading books and newspapers	15
Writing stories, poems, descriptions	12
Drama, role-play, songs, language games	12
Using audio-visuals, TV, video	11
Communication tasks, problem-solving	10
Excursions with the class	7

Eltis and Low (1985; also quoted in Nunan 1988) asked 445 teachers working within the AMEP to list their preferred teaching activities, the ones they perceived to be most useful. The top five turned out to be:

pair/group work
language games
role play
reading topical articles
Cloze exercises

While the two studies cannot be considered directly comparable, because different activities were enquired about and the teacher and student populations were not directly related, there is already a strong hint that activities valued by teachers were not the same as activities valued by learners. In general, it appeared that the teacher population valued forms of class participation associated with communicative teaching, while the student population valued more traditional forms of activity, with more structured modes of participation – including structured conversations, which might have meant teacher-led conversations. As with the private language-school clients in the UK, games and drama and musical activities were low-rated, but provoked disagreement among the student population; however, they were highly regarded by the teachers.

Further investigation of preferences among the student population was conducted by Willing (1985) (referred to earlier in the chapter). This investigation was analysed in terms of individual learning style or personality differences. Willing's study reveals a wide variety of student preferences, and the existence of this variety is an important argument to be taken into account when evaluating the apparent mismatch between teacher and student opinions of teaching and learning activities. Nevertheless, the differences may influence the progress of lessons considerably. Nunan himself (1988: 91) conducted a study of sixty teachers, enquiring about the students' most and least popular activities from the study by Willing. The ratings given by the teachers were then compared to the ratings obtained from the students. In this way, one of the difficulties inherent in comparing the results of the Eltis and Low and Alcorso and Kalantzis studies was avoided. Both sets of participants were asked about the same set of activities. It should be noted, however, that the teachers were not necessarily the teachers of the same students as in the Willing study: this was relatively large-scale survey work, not an ethnographic study of students and teachers in the same classrooms. Therefore the possibility of a teacher carrying his or her particular students through an activity that was otherwise not popular was not investigated. Nunan's results, however, showed that there was a considerable degree of divergence in the values associated with the activities by the two groups. The ratings were given in terms of seven scale points of value; very high/high/medium high/medium/low medium/low/very low.

On five of the activities the ratings were only different by one scale point:

Activity	Students	Teachers
Conversation practice	Very high	Very high
Explanations in class	Very high	High
Vocabulary development	Very high	High
Language games	Very low	Low
Using visuals	Low	Low medium

On two others, the divergence was three scale points:

Pronunciation practice	Very high	Medium
Using audio cassettes	Low	Medium high

On three, the divergence was as much as six scale points:

Error correction	Very high	Low
Student error discovery	Low	Very high
Pair-work	Low	Very high

Clearly, even if the consistent but small difference in the valuations of the first five activities is ignored, there is a strong difference in beliefs concerning the value of certain teaching activities and certain student and teacher roles. Students wanted more pronunciation practice than teachers wanted to give, and less time listening to audio cassettes; they wanted the teachers to correct their errors and the teachers wanted them to discover their errors for themselves; and the teachers' devotion to pair-work was not received with enthusiasm by the students. Because this was questionnaire data, there is no further clue as to the reasons for these valuations: it can only be guessed whether the students' antipathy for pair-work was due to experience of poorly organized sessions, or to embarrassment at speaking to fellow-students in the target language, or a more general attitude devaluing their fellow students as a legitimate resource for language practice.

This kind of research leaves open a number of details which would otherwise be needed, because of the beguiling simplicity of the questions and the ratings. For example, the error correction issue is quite complicated: we do not know from this kind of data whether the students or the teacher were referring to the same phase of error correction – location, identification, supplying the correct form, eliciting the correct form from another class member, and so on. There are no details about the kind of pair-work preferred or dispreferred – for example, involving practice following a model dialogue or the creation of language for an information or opinion gap exercise. Another difficulty is that ratings of value from different groups of teachers produce, not surprisingly, inconsistent results. Nunan's teachers rated language games 'low', but Eltis and Low rated them in the top five 'most valuable'. As Willing's study reminds us that student opinions are quite variable, so should we remember that teachers' are as well. The language classroom is plainly a many-faceted context in which a variety of views about teaching and learning, and the activities constituting that context, compete.

Patterns of attention

An obvious feature of student behaviour which is affected by this rich and confusing classroom context is the attention paid to what is going on in the class and what is intended by the teacher. A series of small-scale studies by Cohen and some of his graduate students has begun to investigate this issue (Cohen, 1992). In one technique, he videotaped students in class, selected interesting moments, and asked them to replay what they remembered attending to at the time. They reported varying the degree to which they ignored or listened to what the other members of the class were saying because of their evaluations of how the students were talking, in terms of speed and comprehensibility. It is not surprising that students do not value interactional practice as highly as their teachers might when they behave selectively as recipients or listeners, and inconsiderately as active participants. Another technique, valued more highly by Cohen, involved stopping the class at selected points to gather responses on four questions: about immediate thoughts, background thoughts, reasons for not paying attention, and work-related activities (Cohen and Hosenfeld, 1983). It was found that student attention levels varied with age (senior citizens averaged 25 per cent of the time) and lesson focus, with an average of 50 per cent of the students actually attending at the moment of stopping the progress of the class. Students who were 'tuning out' – not paying attention – gave a variety of answers as to what they were doing instead:

- evaluating the teacher or fellow students
- thinking about social or academic issues
- thinking about unrelated topics.

Instructional content has to compete, of course, with the active contents of the student's mind for space. When students were attending, the major mode was repeating material to themselves rather than anything more manipulative such as labelling or thinking of an original example or paraphrase. The few who said they were paraphrasing usually meant translating. In view of this unsurprising and very human classroom context – but nevertheless one that is rather ignored by the tidy world of lesson plans and published materials – the generally expressed wish for error identification and correction by the teacher has to be viewed with circumspection.

A student of Cohen's, Alamari (reported by Cohen, 1992: 61), apparently found that 80 per cent of a group of learners of Hebrew as a second language did claim, in post-lesson interviews, that they paid attention to error correction, mostly repeating what was said, but only 15 per cent said they actually wrote it down. Another student, Rosenstein (also reported by Cohen, 1992: 61), ingeniously isolated, for each student, an error for which they had received direct corrective feedback and one for which they had not. The first category were 'public' errors, the second 'secret' errors. Each student's 'secret' error – one that the student was apparently unaware of and had not received direct correction for – was somebody else's 'public' error. In this way there was a possibility of comparing the efficacy of direct correction with other-correction, correction offered to a fellow student. Rosenstein was only able to look at eight students. In the event, about half of the public errors improved during the course and about a fifth of secret ones. If this result were replicated with a larger number of students, it would mean that direct error correction was only about 50 per cent effective in terms of learning outcome – not impressive, but not surprising in view of other studies – and that the learning outcome for a student observing other students being corrected for errors which they also made was very small. Students appear to act – sometimes – on direct feedback to themselves, but 'tune out' on feedback offered to other students. No attempt is reported in this study to compare different kinds of feedback mode.

However, corrective feedback normally comes from the teacher. As such, the relatively low effectiveness of feedback directed at oneself or another student is part of a wider pattern of selective attention. From work by Slimani (1989), it appears that students tend to pay more attention to what fellow-students say than to what teachers say. She studied transcripts of six audio-recorded lessons and 'an exhaustive list of all the items claimed [by the students] to have been encountered and the authors of those claims'. In the first place, most of what students claimed to have learned had been treated publicly in a focused manner by the teachers; but the teachers had treated nearly twice as many topics and issues as the students reported. So, a substantial proportion of what teachers put into the classes was not recalled by the students. In the second place, Slimani found that topics that were raised by students, although far fewer in number, had a far greater chance of being 'taken up' by students, i.e. claimed as part of the instructional content of the lesson. On her figures, a topicalization by the teacher had an even chance of being recalled, one by a fellow-student a three to one chance. Also, the number of students reporting something said by the teacher was rather smaller than the number of students reporting something said by a student. So, the topicalizations by students (usually but not exclusively clarification requests) were more salient and more widely attended to, although presumably intended for individual help, than topicalizations by teachers, although intended for whole-class consumption.

There is possibly a difference here between the work on attention and the work on recall: by and large, in the Cohen studies, peer language and correction offered to peers was 'tuned out' for various reasons; in the

Slimani study a greater proportion of peer talk than of teacher talk received attention. This difference could arise from a number of sources, which at the moment cannot be identified. It could reflect the educational cultures involved (non-natives learning Hebrew in Israel, Algerian students learning English in their own country). It might result from the difference in research techniques, which would suggest that how students say their attention is directed during class is different from the products of their attentional patterns. In fact, Slimani used a post-task questionnaire in which the majority of students ranked input provided by the teacher as the most important; but evidently they did not quite behave congruently. It might reflect the difference in tasks – receiving teacher correction is a more specific form of activity than attending to the general flow of topics around the class, and could be regarded as risking exposure and loss of face. It might be only apparent, since correction offered to peers (as in the Rosenstein study) and topicalization by peers (as in the Slimani study) are different: perhaps students pay attention to the latter but not the former aspects of what their peers are doing in class.

However caused, this variation in attention pattern highlights the importance of information revealed about themselves by students in understanding how classroom participation and work involvement affect what students learn and how that learning is regulated. A further issue pointed up by Slimani has been referred to as the problem of the 'silent student': teachers never know, at least not until test results come in, whether a student who does not overtly participate is using the lesson time productively. In Slimani's study, more claims for uptake of their peers' talk were made by pupils who did not contribute much to the flow of interaction in the classroom than by those who did – suggesting that while peer talk is paid proportionately more attention to than teacher talk, it is mostly the non-talkers who derive most benefit. This unequal distribution of contribution and benefit within a classroom community clearly has important implications for methodology in respect of the opportunities and limitations for student initiation of talk.

Several individual diary or case studies have also commented on this point. Schumann and Schumann (1980) referred to a reluctance to contribute to the class and a preference for 'eavesdropping'. McDonough and McDonough's (1993) subject Q was silent in the class to the point of causing distress to the teachers, and yet revealed in subsequent diary writing and interview how his language and his processing capacity had been growing. Schmidt and Frota's (1986) report of R's learning Portuguese in class in Brazil recognizes the value of the class and of instruction as a linguistic resource, but cannot compare the value of eavesdropping with interaction because of lack of data on language addressed to or initiated by other members of the group. Incidentally, R's diary vividly reveals his reactions to his teacher's intentions and the conflicts he experienced between those and his own preconceptions (Schmidt and Frota, 1986: 243):

> I ... went to the new class, which was already in session ... when I sat down, a drill was in progress. *Ser* [= 'to be'] again, which must be every teacher's lesson one. Teacher asks, student responds: *Você é americana?* ['Are you an American?'] *Sou, sim* ['I am, yes']. When it was my turn the question was *Você é casado?* ['Are you married?'], so I said *não*. L corrected me: *sou, sim*. I objected: *eu não sou casado*. L said [in English], 'We are practising affirmative answers.' I objected again, I'm not married, and L said, 'These questions have nothing to do with real life.' My blood was boiling, but I shut up. . . . (Schmidt and Frota, 1986: 243)

In this section we have seen that individuals learning in classrooms may be more or less skilled at obtaining the language resources – the input – that they need, and operate various kinds of regulatory devices, like attention and participation. Observation of a class in action may not reveal the complexity of the interaction between the different participants' agendas, though it will reveal the linguistic and social interaction. However, it is clear that learning outcomes depend on those agendas, rather than on the observable facts of the linguistic input or the distribution of active participation alone. Techniques of self-revelation, however imperfect, allow this complexity to be appreciated; one role for learner training is to increase the individual learner's benefit from being a member of a classroom learning group.

Evaluation

In attempts to evaluate language-teaching programmes, it is commonplace to use language achievement data – usually gain scores on some test – as one kind of evidence. It would be a foolish evaluator who recommended a particular programme without being able to show that students on it learned at least as well as on some competing kind of programme. However, evaluation requires much else, not least according to its purpose. Brown (1989), writing in general terms about evaluation procedures, presents the following spectrum of evidence, of both quantitative and qualitative kinds (adapted from Brown, 1989: 233, table 1):

Evaluator's role	*Categories*	*Procedures*
Outsider looking in	Existing information	Records analysis
		Systems analysis
		Literature review
		Letter-writing

	Tests	Proficiency Placement Diagnostic Achievement
	Observations	Case studies Diary studies Behaviour Interaction Inventories
Facilitator drawing out information	Interviews	Individual Group
	Meetings	Advisory Interest group Review
	Questionnaire	Biodata surveys Opinion surveys Self-ratings Judgemental ratings

Brown comments that qualitative evidence (mainly collected by the evaluator in the role of a facilitator drawing out information), though perceived as less rigorously scientific, often carries greater weight in the final decisions than quantitative 'facts'.

While the role of student opinion and student classroom behaviour is acknowledged in such schemes as Brown's, the importance of researching process and skill development for programme evaluation has been largely unaddressed. However, McDonough and McDonough's (1993) case-study of a learner in an English for Academic Purposes programme (undertaken before entering his academic Department for doctoral research) highlighted the need for serious consideration of this point, since it revealed how a student who was apparently failing to make progress slowly began to use the resources (language, teachers, and other students) that had been available. An important turning-point, two months after the beginning of his course, was when he said, 'Now I must learn English' – at last a recognition of his problem. In this study, several themes proved to be particularly important:

- the time lag between *mention* of particular linguistic forms or particular strategies and the student's *incorporation* of them in his own learning plans
- the highly selective use made of topics in the syllabus
- the highly restricted modes of practice use
- the apparent inhibition about active participation

- the student's eventual success.

A course is usually not established just for the one person (with some obvious exceptions); nevertheless, the authors argued that the evaluation of a course, and the decisions to be taken about modification of an existing course structure, involve the learning histories – the process – of the number of individuals taking that course. The authors commented (McDonough and McDonough, 1993: 137):

> There is clear evidence here of a mismatch between input and uptake that is both quantitative and qualitative – quantitative in the sense of a considerable timelag between what was offered on the course and its much later acceptance into Q's own learning repertoire, as with the very slow growth of interest in the local environment. The mismatch is also qualitative in the sense that some input is not taken up at all – overt study skills teaching is a case in point – and other elements, such as well-meant advice on learning vocabulary, are taken up much later but without any reference to earlier instruction.

Inevitably, such an approach would require large resources of time and manpower to be feasible in evaluating a programme with large numbers of participants. Elley's (1989: 271) stricture about designing an evaluation like a sledgehammer to crack a nut where expensive and time-consuming methods are employed relating only to a small sample have to be acknowledged. Nevertheless, just as it is clear that learners do not learn all that they are taught, so it is true that learning does not stop when the course finishes.

Summary and conclusions

The relationship between language-learning skills and processes and the classroom outlined here demonstrates that much more needs to be known about both, before truly defensible generalizations and prescriptions for successful class management can be offered. Rather, the implication of process information – the real nature of the relationship between classroom events and learning outcomes – is currently that we are learning how much we do not know, rather than confidently establishing empirically justified generalizations about good practice. In all the areas reviewed –

- the introduction of explicit strategy teaching
- learner training
- the conflict between learners' and teachers' cultural assumptions about classrooms
- the different evaluations by learners and teachers of learning activities
- the value of active participation

- the value of attentional patterns
- the use of process information in evaluating programmes
- the difference in quality and time of input and intake

the questions generate more questions rather than final answers. From the applied linguist's point of view, this is probably a healthy, if frustrating, situation. Healthy, because answers can be restrictive, questions liberating.

What has been developed and continues to expand is a range of investigative techniques which can be used, both by the academic researcher and by teachers themselves, to probe the behaviour, strategic approaches, and beliefs of learners in different situations. These can be used both to evaluate existing features of teaching programmes and suggest innovations and to monitor ways of maintaining those innovations. Research can monitor all sorts of components of the process:

- what learners do with the language material they encounter
- what patterns of participation are valued and how
- what kinds of encounters with the language are productive
- what education of the learners in the methods, and what education of the teachers about the learners, is appropriate and effective
- and, ultimately, which kinds of change in the learners can be attributed to which features of their language programmes.

References

ABRAHAMS, R. G. and VANN, R. J. 1987: Strategies of two language learners: a case study. In Wenden and Rubin (1987: 103–18).

ALDERSON, J. C. 1984: Reading in a foreign language: a reading problem or a language problem? In Alderson, J. C. and Urquhart, A. S. (eds), *Reading in a foreign language*. Harlow: Longman, 1–27.

—— and CLAPHAM, C. (eds) 1992: *Examining the ELTS Test: an account of the first stage of the ELTS revision project*. ELTS research report 2. British Council/University of Cambridge Local Examinations Syndicate/International Development Program of Australian Universities and Colleges.

—— and WALL, D. 1993: Does washback exist? *Applied Linguistics* 14(2), 115–29.

ALLWRIGHT, D. and BAILEY, K. 1991: *Focus on the language classroom*. Cambridge: Cambridge University Press.

ALVAREZ DE GALICIA, M. G. 1989: *Reading in English for Academic Purposes (EAP): the effect of background knowledge with special reference to schema-directed processes*. Unpublished Ph.D., University of Edinburgh. Dissertation Abstracts No. AAC D 91654.

ANDERSON, A. and LYNCH, T. 1989: *Listening*. Oxford: Oxford University Press.

ANDERSON, J. R. 1983: *The architecture of cognition*. Cambridge, Mass.: Harvard University Press.

ANDERSON, N. J., BACHMAN, L., PERKINS, K., and COHEN, A. 1991: An exploratory study into the construct validity of a reading comprehension test: triangulation of data sources. *Language Testing* 8(1), 41–66.

ARNDT, V. 1987: Six writers in search of texts: a protocol based study of L1 and L2 writing. *English Language Teaching Journal* 41, 257–67.

—— and WHITE, R. 1991: *Process writing*. Harlow: Longman.

ASLANIAN, Y. 1985: Investigating the reading problems of English as a second language students: an alternative. *English Language Teaching Journal* 39(1), 20–7.

BAILEY, K. M. 1980: An introspective analysis of an individual's language learning experience. In Krashen, S. K. and Scarcella, R. (eds), *Research in second language acquisition*. Rowley, Mass.: Newbury House, 58–67.

—— and OCHSNER, R. 1983: A methodological review of the diary studies: windmill tilting or social science? In Bailey, K. M., Long, M., and Peck, S. (eds), *Second language acquisition studies*. Rowley, Mass.: Newbury House, 188–98.

BALLARD, B. 1984: Improving student writing: an integrated approach to cultural adjustment. In Williams, R., Swales, J., and Kirkman, J. (eds), *Common ground: shared interests in ESP and communication studies*. ELT Documents 118. London: Pergamon/British Council.

BARTLETT, F. 1958: *Thinking: an experimental and social study*. London: George Allen & Unwin.

BELIAEV, B. V. 1963: *The psychology of teaching foreign languages*. Trans. R. F. Hingley. Oxford: Oxford University Press.

BERKENKOTTER, C. 1983: Decisions and revisions: the planning strategies of a publishing writer. *College composition and communication* 34(2), 156–69.

BEVER, T. G. 1970: The cognitive basis for linguistic structures. In Hayes, J. R. (ed.), *Cognition and the development of language*. New York: Wiley, 279–352.

BIALYSTOK, E. 1990: *Communication Strategies*. Oxford: Blackwell.

BLOCK, E. 1986: The comprehension strategies of second language readers. *TESOL Quarterly* 20(3), 463–94.

BLOOR, M. and BLOOR, T. 1989: Cultural expectations and sociopragmatic failure in academic writing. In Adams, P., Heaton, J. B., and Howarth, P. (eds), *Socio-cultural issues in EAP*. Modern English Publications in association with British Council, Developments in ELT. London: Macmillan, 1–12.

BOSSERS, B. 1991: On thresholds, ceilings, and short circuits: the relation between L1 reading, L2 reading, and L2 knowledge. In Hulstijn, J. H. and Matter, J. F. (eds), *Reading in two languages*. Association Internationale de Linguistique Appliquée Review 8, 45–60.

BROWN, J. D. 1989: Language program evaluation: a synthesis of existing possibilities. In Johnson (1989: 222–41).

BUCK, G. 1991: The testing of listening comprehension: an introspective study. *Language Testing* 8(1), 67–91.

CANALE, M. and SWAIN, M. 1980: Theoretical bases of communicative approaches to second language teaching and testing. *Applied Linguistics* 1(1), 1–47.

CARRELL, P. L. 1984: Schema theory and ESL reading: classroom implications and applications. *Modern Language Journal* 68(4), 332–43.

1989: Metacognitive awareness and second language reading. *Modern Language Journal* 73(2), 121–34.

1991: Second language reading: reading ability or language proficiency? *Applied Linguistics* 12(2), 159–79.

and EISTERHOLD, J. C. 1983: Schema theory and ESL reading pedagogy. *TESOL Quarterly* 17(4), 553–73.

PHARIS, B. G. and LIBERTO, J. C. 1989: Metacognitive strategy training for ESL reading. *TESOL Quarterly* 23(4), 647–78.

CARROLL, J. B. and SAPON, S. 1959: *Modern language aptitude test*. New York: Psychological Corporation.

CARROLL, B. J. and WEST, R. 1989: *The English Speaking Union framework*. Harlow: Longman.

CHAMOT, A.-U. 1987: The learning strategies of ESL students. In Wenden and Rubin (1987: 71–84).

CLARKE, M. 1979: The short-circuit hypothesis of ESL reading – or when language competence interferes with reading performance. *Modern Language Journal* 64(2), 203–9.

COHEN, A. D. 1984: On taking language tests: what students report. *Language Testing* 1, 70–81.

1987: Student processing of feedback on their compositions. In Wenden and Rubin (1987: 57–69).

1991: Feedback on writing: the use of verbal report. *Studies in Second Language Acquisition* 13, 133–59.

1992: *Language learning*. Rowley, Mass.: Newbury House.

and APHEK, E. 1981: Easifying second language learning. *Studies in Second Language Acquisition* 3(2), 221–36.

and CAVALCANTI, M. C. 1987: Giving and getting feedback on compositions: a comparison of teacher and student verbal report. *Evaluation and Research in Education* 1(2), 63–73.

1990: Feedback on compositions: teacher and student verbal reports. In Kroll (1990a: 155–77).

GLASMAN, H., ROSENBAUM-COHEN, P. R., FERRARA, J., and FINE, J. 1979: Reading English for specialized purposes: discourse analysis and the use of student informants. *TESOL Quarterly* 13(4), 551–64.

and HOSENFELD, C. 1983: Some views of mentalistic data in second language research. *Language Learning* 31(2), 285–313.

and OLSHTAIN, E. 1992: The production of speech acts by EFL learners. *Proceedings of the 10th Conference of the Academic Committee for Research on Language Testing (ACROLT)*, Kiryat Anavim, Israel, May 1991, 1–18.

and ROBBINS, M. 1976: Toward assessing interlanguage performance: the relationship between selected errors, learners' characteristics, and learners' expectations. *Language Learning* 26(1), 45–66.

CONNOR, U. and McCAGG, P. 1983: Cross-cultural differences and perceived quality in written paraphrases of English expository prose. *Applied Linguistics* 4(3), 259–68.

COOK, V. J. 1989: Universal grammar theory and the classroom. *System* 17(2), 169–82.

1991: *Second language learning and language teaching*. Sevenoaks: Edward Arnold.

COOPER, M. 1984: Linguistic competence of practised and unpractised non-native readers of English. In Alderson, J. C. and Urquhart, A. (eds), *Reading in a foreign language*. Harlow: Longman, 122–35.

COOPER, M. and HOLZMANN, M. 1983: Talking about protocols. *College Composition and Communication* 34(3), 282–93.

CORDER, S. P. 1967: The significance of learners' errors. *International Review of Applied Linguistics* 5(4), 161–70.

CROOKES, G. 1989: Planning and interlanguage variation. *Studies in Second Language Acquisition* 11, 367–83.

CURRAN, C. A. 1976: *Counseling-learning in second languages*. Apple River, Ill.: Apple River Press.

DEVINE, J., CARRELL, P. L., and ESKEY, D. E. (eds) 1987: *Research in reading English as a second language*. Washington, DC: TESOL.

DICKINSON, L. 1987: *Self-instruction in language learning*. Cambridge: Cambridge University Press.

DOLLERUP, C., GLAHN, E., and HANSEN, C. R. 1982: Reading strategies and test-taking techniques in an EFL reading comprehension test: a preliminary report. *Journal of Applied Language Study* 1(1), 93–9.

EFL SERVICES LTD 1992: *Students talking*. Elsworthy: EFL Services Ltd.

ELLEY, W. B. 1989: Tailoring the evaluation to fit the context. In Johnson (1989: 270–86).

ELLIS, G. and SINCLAIR, B. 1989: *Learning to learn English*. Cambridge: Cambridge University Press.

ELLIS, R. 1986: *Understanding second language acquisition*. Oxford: Oxford University Press.

ERICSON, K. A. 1988: Concurrent verbal reports on text comprehension: a review. *Text* 8, 295–325.

    and SIMON, H. A. 1987: Verbal reports on thinking. In Faerch and Kasper (1987: 24–53).

ESKEY, D. 1988: Holding in the bottom: an interactive approach to the language problems of second language readers. In Carrell, P. L., Devine, J., and Eskey, D. (eds), *Interactive approaches to second language reading*. Cambridge: Cambridge University Press, 93–100.

FAERCH, C. and KASPER, G. (eds) 1983a: *Strategies in interlanguage communication*. Harlow: Longman.

    1983b: Plans and strategies in foreign language communication. In Faerch and Kasper (1983a: 20–60).

    (eds) 1987: *Introspection in second language research*. Clevedon: Multilingual Matters.

FAIGLEY, L. and WITTE, S. 1981: Analysing revision. *College Composition and Communication* 32, 400–14.

FAIRFAX, O. and GREEN, M. 1989: Introspection, language learning, and curriculum development. *System* 17(1), 71–82.

FATHMAN, A. and WHALLEY, E. 1990: Teacher response to student writing: focus on form versus content. In Kroll (1990a: 179–90).

FELDMAN, U. and STEMMER, B. 1987: Thin____ aloud a____ retrospective da____ in C-te____ taking: diff____ languages – diff____ learners – sa____ approaches. In Faerch and Kasper (1987: 251–66).

FLOWER, L. 1979: Writer-based prose: a cognitive basis for problems in writing. *College English* 41(1), 19–37.

    and HAYES, J. R. 1980: The cognition of discovery: defining a rhetorical problem. *College Composition and Communication* 31(1), 21–32.

    1981: A cognitive process theory of writing. *College Composition and Communication* 32(3), 365–87.

FLOYD, J. 1988: *Study skills for higher education: a use of English course*. Harlow: Longman.

FLYNN, S. 1989: The role of the head-initial/head-final parameter in the acquisition of English relative clauses by adult Spanish and Japanese speakers. In Gass and Schachter (1989: 89–108).

FRIEDLANDER, A. 1990: Composing in English: effects of a first language on writing in English as a second language. In Kroll (1990a: 109–25).

FURRY, N. M. 1990: *Explorations in extra textual space: reading comprehension in a foreign language*. Unpublished Ph.D., University of Texas at Austin. Dissertation Abstracts No. AAC 9105549.

GALVAN, M. 1985: *The writing process of Spanish speaking bilingual/bicultural graduate students: an ethnographic perspective*. Unpublished Ph.D., University of Hofstra. Dissertation Abstracts No. AAC 8606928.

GASKILL, W. H. 1986: *Revising in Spanish and English as a second language: a process-oriented study of composition.* Unpublished Ph.D., University of California at Los Angeles. Dissertation Abstracts No. AAC 8702654.

GASS, S. M. and SCHACHTER, J. (eds) 1989: *Linguistic perspectives on second language acquisition.* Cambridge: Cambridge University Press.

GILLETTE, B. 1987: Two successful learners: an introspective approach. In Faerch and Kasper (1987: 267–79).

GROTJAHN, R. 1987: On the methodological basis of introspective methods. In Faerch and Kasper (1987: 54–81).

HAASTRUP, K. and PHILLIPSON, R. 1983: Achievement strategies in learner/native speaker interaction. In Faerch and Kasper (1983a: 140–58).

HALIMAH, A. M. 1991: *EST writing, rhetorically processed and produced: a case study of Kuwaiti learners.* Unpublished Ph.D., University of Essex, D 95798.

HAMP-LYONS, E. 1990: Second language writing: assessment issues. In Kroll (1990a: 68–87).

HANSEN, L. and STANSFIELD, C. 1981: The relationship of field-dependent-independent cognitive styles to foreign language achievement. *Language Learning* 31(2), 349–67.

HAYES, J. R. and FLOWER, L. S. 1983: Uncovering cognitive processes in writing: an introduction to protocol analysis. In Mosenthal, P., Tamor, S., and Walmsley, S. (eds), *Research on writing: principles and methods.* Harlow: Longman, 207–19.

HOOSHMAND, D. 1984: *The organisation of prose and its effects on reading English as a foreign language.* Unpublished Ph.D., University of Illinois. Dissertation Abstracts No. AAC 8422082.

HOPKINS, D. 1993: *A teacher's guide to classroom research,* 2nd edn. Oxford: Oxford University Press.

HORWITZ, E. K. 1987: Surveying beliefs about language learning. In Wenden and Rubin (1987: 119–32).

HOSENFELD, C. 1976: Learning about learning: discovering our students' strategies. *Foreign Language Annals* 9(2), 117–29.

1979: Cora's view of learning grammar. *Canadian Modern Language Review* 35, 602–7.

1984: Case studies of ninth grade readers. In Alderson, J. C. and Urquhart, A. S. (eds), *Reading in a foreign language.* Harlow: Longman, 231–44.

HUEY, E. B. 1968: *The psychology and pedagogy of reading.* Cambridge, Mass.: Massachusetts Institute of Technology Press. (Originally published 1908.)

HUGHES, A. 1989: *Testing for language teachers.* Cambridge: Cambridge University Press.

JAMES, K. 1984: The writing of theses by speakers of EFL: the results of a case study. In Williams, R., Swales, J., and Kirkman, J. (eds), *Common ground: shared interests in ESP and communication studies.* ELT Documents 118. London: Pergamon/British Council, 99–113.

JOHNSON, C. V. 1985: *The composing process of six ESL students.* Unpublished Ph.D., University of Illinois. Dissertation Abstracts No. AAC 8514773.

JOHNSON, R. K. (ed.) 1989: *The second language curriculum.* Cambridge: Cambridge University Press.

JONES, S. and TETROE, J. 1987: Composing in a second language. In Matsuhashi, A. (ed.), *Writing in real time.* Norwood, NJ: Ablex, 34–57.

KASPER, G. and DAHL, M. 1991: Research methods in interlanguage pragmatics. *Studies in Second Language Acquisition* 13, 215–47.

KERN, R. G. 1988: *The role of comprehension strategies in foreign language reading.* Unpublished Ph.D., University of California, Berkeley. Dissertation Abstracts No. AAC 8902150.

1989: Second language reading strategy instruction: its effects on comprehension and word inference ability. *Modern Language Journal* 73(2), 135–49.

KRAPELS, A. R. 1990: An overview of second language writing process research. In Kroll (1990*a*: 37–56).

KRASHEN, S. 1977: Some issues relating to the Monitor Model. In Brown, H. D., Yorio, C., and Crymes, R. (eds), *On TESOL '77: teaching and learning English as a second language; trends in research and practice.* Washington, DC: TESOL, 144–58.

1982: *Principles and practice in second language acquisition.* Oxford: Pergamon.

KROLL, B. (ed.) 1990*a*: *Second language writing: research insights for the classroom.* Cambridge: Cambridge University Press.

1990*b*: What does time buy? ESL student performance on home versus class compositions. In Kroll (1990*a*: 140–54).

LARSEN-FREEMAN, D. and LONG, M. H. 1991: *An introduction to second language acquisition research.* Harlow: Longman.

LAY, N. D. S. 1982: Composing processes of adult ESL learners: a case study. *TESOL Quarterly* 16(3), 406.

VAN LIER, L. 1989: Reeling, writhing, drawling, stretching, and fainting in coils: oral proficiency interviews and conversation. *TESOL Quarterly* 23(3), 489–508.

LITTLEWOOD, W. T. 1984: *Foreign and second language learning: language acquisition research and its implications for the classroom.* Cambridge: Cambridge University Press.

LONG, M. H. and CROOKES, G. 1986: *Intervention points in second language classroom processes.* Working papers 5, 2, Department of English as a Second Language, University of Hawaii at Manoa.

LUNZER, E. and GARDNER, E. 1979: *The effective use of reading.* London: Heinemann.

MACHADO, M. C. 1985: *Reading in L₂: an investigation of the role of background knowledge or schemata in comprehension.* Unpublished Ph.D., University of Georgetown. Dissertation Abstracts No. AAC 8613942.

MACLENNAN, C. 1987: An investigation of the criteria which a group of Hong Kong and Macau students of English list as those which make a good teacher. *Proceedings of the Institute of Language in Education 3rd International Seminar* (Dec.), on 'Languages in Education in a Bilingual or Multilingual situation', 61–74.

McDONOUGH, J. E. 1978: *Listening to lectures: Sociology, Biology, Government, Computing, Mechanics.* Oxford: Oxford University Press.

and McDONOUGH, S. H. 1993: From EAP to chemistry: risking the anecdotal. In Blue, G. M. (ed.), *Language, learning, and success: studying through English.* Modern English Publications/British Council. London: Macmillan, 132–40.

McDONOUGH, S. H. 1981: *Psychology in foreign language teaching.* London: Allen & Unwin. 2nd edn. 1986.

(forthcoming): Protocol analysis of summary writing processes used by students of English for academic purposes.

McLAUGHLIN, B. 1978: The Monitor Model: some methodological considerations. *Language Learning* 28, 309–32.

1987: *Theories of second language learning.* Sevenoaks: Edward Arnold.

MONTEIRO, QUEIROZ DE MELO, S. 1992 *A contrastive investigation or 'reading strategy awareness' and 'reading strategy use' by adolescents reading in the first language (Portuguese) and in the foreign language (English).* Unpublished Ph.D., University of Essex. Dissertation Abstracts No. D 98258.

MURPHY, J. M. 1985: Examining ESL listening as an interpretive language process. *TESOL Newsletter* (Dec.), 23–4.

NAIMAN, N., FRÖHLICH, M., STERN, H. H., and TODESCO, A. 1978: *The good language learner.* Research in Education Series 7. Toronto, Ontario: Ontario Institute for Studies in Education.

NEVILLE, M. H. and PUGH, A. K. 1976–7: Content in reading and listening: variations in approach to Cloze tasks. *Reading Research Quarterly* 12(1), 13–31.

NEVO, N. 1989: Test-taking strategies on a multiple choice test of reading comprehension. *Language Testing* 6(2), 199–215.

NEWELL, A. and SIMON, H. 1972: *Human problem solving.* Englewood Cliffs, NJ: Prentice Hall.

NISBETT, R. E. and WILSON, T. D. 1977: Telling more than we can know: verbal reports on mental processes. *Psychological Review* 84, 231–59.

NUNAN, D. 1988: *The learner-centred curriculum.* Cambridge; Cambridge University Press.

1992: *Research methods in language learning.* Cambridge: Cambridge University Press.

NUTTALL, C. 1982: *Teaching reading skills in a foreign language.* Practical Language Teaching 9. London: Heinemann.

OLSHAVSKY, J. E. 1976–7: Reading as problem solving: an investigation of strategies. *Reading Research Quarterly* 12(4), 654–74.

OLSHTAIN, E. and COHEN, A. D. 1989: Speech act behaviour across languages. In Dechert, H. W. and Raupach, R. (eds), *Transfer in language production.* Norwood, NJ: Ablex, 53–67.

1990: The learning of complex speech act behaviour. *TESL Canada Journal/Revue TESL du Canada* 7(2), 45–65.

OLSON, G. M., DUFFY, S. A. and MACK, R. L. 1984: Think-out-loud as a method for studying real-time comprehension processes. In Kieras, D. E. and Just, M. A. (eds), *New methods in reading comprehension research.* Hillsdale, NJ: Lawrence Erlbaum, 253–86.

O'MALLEY, J. M. 1987: The effects of training in the use of learning strategies on acquiring English as a second language. In Wenden and Rubin (1987: 133–44).

and CHAMOT, A.-U. 1990: *Learning strategies in second language acquisition.* Cambridge: Cambridge University Press.

CHAMOT, A.-U. and KÜPPER, L. 1989: Listening comprehension strategies in second language acquisition. *Applied Linguistics* 10(4), 418–35.

CHAMOT, A.-U., STEWNER-MANZANARES, G., RUSSO, R. P., and KÜPPER, L. 1985a: Learning strategy applications with students of English as a second language. *TESOL Quarterly* 19(3), 557–84.

CHAMOT, A.-U., STEWNER-MANZANARES, G., KÜPPER, L., and RUSSO, R. P. 1985b: Learning strategies used by beginning and intermediate ESL students. *Language Learning* 35(1), 21–46.

OSKARSON, M. 1984: *Self-assessment of foreign language skills*. Strasburg: Council of Europe.

OXFORD, R. L. 1990: *Language learning strategies: what every teacher should know*. New York: Newbury House/Harper & Row.

CROOKALL, D., COHEN, A. D., LAVINE, R., NYIKOS, M., and SUTTER, W. 1990: Strategy training for language learners: six situational case studies and a training model. *Foreign Language Annals* 22(3), 197–216.

PALMER, H. E. 1964: *The principles of language study*. Oxford: Oxford University Press. (First published by Harrap 1922.)

PERL, S. 1980: Understanding composing. *College Composition and Communication* 31(4), 363–9.

1981: *Coding the composing process: a guide for teachers and researchers*. Manuscript written for the National Institute of Education, Washington, DC. ED 240609.

PICKETT, G. D. 1978: *The foreign language learning process*. London: British Council English Teaching Information Centre.

POLITZER, R. and McGROARTY, M. 1985: An exploratory study of learning behaviours and their relationship to gains in linguistic and communicative competence. *TESOL Quarterly* 19(1), 103–23.

POULISSE, N., BONGAERTS, T., and KELLERMAN, E. 1987: The use of retrospective verbal reports in the analysis of compensatory strategies. In Faerch and Kasper (1987: 213–29).

PRABHU, N. S. 1987: *Second language pedagogy*. Oxford: Oxford University Press.

PRITCHARD, R. 1990: The effects of cultural schemata on reading processing strategies. *Reading Research Quarterly* 25, 273–95.

RADECKI, P. M. and SWALES, J. M. 1988: ESL student reaction to written comments on their written work. *System* 16(3), 355–66.

RAIMES, A. 1985: What unskilled ESL students do as they write; a classroom study of composing. *TESOL Quarterly* 19, 229–58.

1987: Language proficiency, writing ability, and composing strategies: a study of ESL college student writers. *Language Learning* 37(3), 439–67.

REID, J. 1990: Responding to different topic types: a quantitative analysis from a contrastive rhetoric perspective. In Kroll (1990*a*: 191–210).

RORSCHACH, E. G. 1986: *The effects of reader awareness: a case study of three ESL student writers*. Unpublished Ph.D., University of New York. Dissertation Abstracts No. AAC 8706333.

RUBIN, J. 1975: What the good language learner can teach us. *TESOL Quarterly* 9, 41–51.

SARIG, G. 1987: High level reading in the first and the foreign language: some comparative process data. In Devine, J., Carrell, P. L., and Eskey, D. E. (eds), *Research in reading English as a second language*. Washington, DC: TESOL, 107–20.

SCHMIDT, R. 1983: Interaction, acculturation, and the acquisition of communicative competence. In Wolfson, N. and Judd, E. (eds), *Sociolinguistics and second language acquisition*. Rowley, Mass.: Newbury House.

and FROTA, S. N. 1986: Developing basic conversational ability in a second language: a case study of an adult learner of Portuguese. In Day, R. (ed.), *Talking to learn: conversation in second language acquisition*. Rowley, Mass.: Newbury House, 237–326.

SCHUMANN, F. and SCHUMANN, J. H. 1980: Diary of a language learner: a further analysis. In Krashen, S. K. and Scarcella, R. (eds), *Research in second language acquisition*. Rowley, Mass.: Newbury House, 55–7.

SELIGER, H. W. and SHOHAMY, E. 1989: *Second language learning research methods*. Oxford: Oxford University Press.

SELINKER, L. 1972: Interlanguage. *International Review of Applied Linguistics* 10(3), 201–31.

SKEHAN, P. 1989: *Individual differences in second language learning*. Sevenoaks: Edward Arnold.

1992: *Second language acquisition strategies and task-based learning*. Working Papers. Department of EFL, Thames Valley University.

SLIMANI, A. 1989: The role of topicalization in classroom language learning. *System* 17(2), 223–34.

SMAGORINSKY, P. 1989: The reliability and validity of protocol analysis. *Written Communication* 6(4), 463–79.

SOMMERS, A. 1980: Revision strategies of student writers and experienced adult writers. *College Composition and Communication* 31, 378–88.

STEFFENSEN, M. S. 1987: The effect of context and culture on children's L_2 reading: a review. In Devine, J., Carrell, P. L., and Eskey, D. E. (eds), *Research in reading English as a second language*. Washington, DC: TESOL, 43–54.

and JOAG-DEV, C. 1984: Cultural knowledge and reading. In Alderson, J. C. and Urquhart, A. S. (eds), *Reading in a foreign language*. Harlow: Longman, 48–61.

STENHOUSE, L. 1975: *Introduction to curriculum research and development*. London: Heinemann.

STERN, H. H. 1975: What can we learn from the good language learner? *Canadian Modern Language Review* 31, 304–18.

TARONE, E. 1977: Conscious communication strategies in interlanguage. In Brown, H. D., Yorio, C., and Crymes, R. (eds), *On TESOL '77: teaching and learning English as a second language: trends in research and practice*. Washington, DC: TESOL, 194–203.

1980: Communication strategies, foreigner talk, and repair in interlanguage. *Language Learning* 30, 417–31.

1981: Some thoughts on the notion of 'communication strategy'. *TESOL Quarterly* 15(3), 285–95.

THORNDIKE, E. 1917: Reading as reasoning. *Journal of Educational Psychology* 8, 323–32.

URQUHART, A. 1984: The effect of rhetorical ordering on readability. In Alderson, J. C. and Urquhart, A. S. (eds), *Reading in a foreign language*. Harlow: Longman, 160–75.

VARADI, T. 1980: Strategies of target language learner communication: message adjustment. *International Review of Applied Linguistics* 18, 59–71.

WALKER, R. 1985: *Doing research: a handbook for teachers*. London: Methuen.

WEINER, B. 1972: *Theories of motivation: from mechanism to cognition*. Chicago: Markham.

WENDEN, A. L. 1986: Helping L_2 learners think about learning. *English Language Teaching Journal* 40, 3–12.

1987: Incorporating learner training in the classroom. In Wenden and Rubin (1987: 159–68).

and RUBIN, J. (eds), 1987: *Learner strategies in language learning*. Hemel Hempstead: Prentice Hall International English Language Teaching.

WHITE, L. 1986: Implication of parametric variation for adult second language acquisition: an investigation of the pro-drop parameter. In Cook, V. J. (ed.), *Experimental approaches to second language acquisition*. Oxford: Pergamon.

WHITE, R. 1993: Saying please: pragmalinguistic problems in the learning of English. Lecture given at the University of Essex.

WILLING, K. 1985: *Learning styles in adult migrant education.* Sydney: New South Wales Adult Migrant Education Service.

1989: *Teaching how to learn: A teachers' guide and activity workshops.* Macquarie University: National Centre for Research in English Language Teaching.

WILLIAMS, E. and MORAN, C. 1989: Reading in a foreign language at intermediate and advanced levels with particular reference to English. *Language Teaching* 22(4), 217–28.

WILLIS, D. 1990: *The lexical syllabus.* London and Glasgow: Collins.

YOUSSEF, O. A. A. 1988: *The effect of two schema based strategies on Egyptian high school students' comprehension of English as a Foreign Language.* Unpublished Ph.D., University of Indiana. Dissertation Abstracts No. AAC 89100155.

ZAMEL, V. 1983: The composing processes of advanced ESL students: six case studies. *TESOL Quarterly* 17, 165–87.

1985: Responding to student writing. *TESOL Quarterly* 19(1), 79–102.

Index